# God Moves

# GOD MOVES

## THE END OF A JOURNEY

## AND THE START OF A PILGRIMAGE

NEIL S. DAVIES

Including: On The Incarnation of the Word by St. Athanasius

*AuthorHouse™ LLC*
*1663 Liberty Drive*
*Bloomington, IN 47403*
*www.authorhouse.com*
*Phone: 1-800-839-8640*



*Published by AuthorHouse 06/25/2013*

*ISBN: 978-1-4817-6012-6 (sc)*
*ISBN: 978-1-4817-6013-3 (hc)*
*ISBN: 978-1-4817-6014-0 (e)*

*Library of Congress Control Number: 2013910161*



*This translation was made by Sister Penelope Lawson, of the Anglican Community of St. Mary the Virgin in Wantage, England. It was originally published with a byline that reads only "Translated and edited by A Religious of C.S.M.V."*

*Reproduced with permission of:*
*CHRISTIAN CLASSICS ETHEREAL LIBRARY*
*www.ccel.org*

To Zulu, Orphan, and Lebanon

You showed me the way,<br>
But I didn't follow.<br>
You spoke His name,<br>
But I didn't listen.<br>
I would, I pray with all my heart,<br>
Be for others what you have been for me.<br>
How I long to speak to you again!

# Part 1

# Contents

# 1

# I Am One of Those

*I may not have gone where I intended to go, but I think I have ended up where I needed to be.*

—DOUGLAS ADAMS

*(The Hitchhiker's Guide to the Galaxy)*

I thought about God for a very long time during a period in my life when thinking about God and trying to fathom the unfathomable were the only things that made sense. But after all that time, I cannot say that I have arrived at an ultimate truth. What I do suspect, however, is that God is not who I thought he was (or should be), and this realization did not come through reflection or thought, but permeated every fiber of my being in an instant nearly twelve years later, when I was surprised by God in a way I never thought possible.

There is an infinite realm of human experiences, and my background and age have allowed me to experience only a few. But these experiences and events have led me in a direction that could have had only one possible destination, and that destination is exactly what I wanted from the beginning: the knowledge that as a unique individual with peculiarities, vulnerabilities, insecurities, wants, needs, desires, likes, and dislikes, I am important to God and worthy of his love. Had I been anyone else, this knowledge would probably have been mine a long time ago, but I am the sort of man who learns best the hard way.

Come to think of it, knowledge based on experience is always better and worth more than knowledge acquired from some other source, and despite experiencing pain and anger and frustration in coming to that knowledge, I prefer it that way. Growth without a measure of suffering and inward reflection isn't growth at all but rather an occurrence the "grower" knows nothing about and probably never will. Something that isn't known cannot be appreciated. To put it another way, an athlete who trains diligently and hard for an upcoming event can feel the pain in his muscles. He can feel his lungs burn and his heart pound inside his chest, and when the day is over, he can say to himself, *I have achieved much today*. Without the exertion, he would have felt that he needed to train harder.

I am also one of those who, from time to time, like to imagine that I am in orbit around the Earth after being magically transported there and, as thoughts and dreams go, I am completely comfortable and can breathe easily in the vacuum of space. It is an almost entirely cloudless day on the part of the planet facing me, and as I look at the Earth, I am suddenly aware that everything I have ever experienced and everybody I have ever known, dead or still alive, are restricted to that planet. The African continent comes into view, and I recognize the familiar shape of the southern tip. *I grew up there,* I say to myself. My eyes drift to the other continents, but I am instinctively drawn to South Africa. As I follow my eyes to the north, the northern tip of Scotland, I say to myself, *What a journey!*

It is said that a journey of a thousand miles starts with a single step. As obvious as this may seem, I think that sometimes we are unaware that we even took a first step. A real journey, an inward journey, is recognized only after the fact; you don't recall the first step, but you are aware of a beginning at some point. Now, after the fact, I recognize the possibility that I may never see things the same way. I know about cause and effect. I know about atoms and molecules bumping into each other. I know that every choice we make signifies the death of all other possibilities in that point in time. However, even Einstein is quoted as saying, "God does not play dice with the universe."

My eyes return to South Africa and Scotland as I'm in quiet orbit around the Earth. Perhaps a roll of the dice, accidental or otherwise, did not cause the seemingly random events I experienced in these two places. Maybe these things happened for a reason—not as a journey for the sake of a journey, but the solidification of moments and memories that will never escape me. These memories evoke within me a longing with such deliberate purpose that I am often unable to conceive how I could have been so blind and selfish and stupid. Alas, I learn best the hard way.

Although my presence in some of these places has long since passed, I am still able to recall everything in the finest detail. When I close my eyes, I can see myself as an eighteen-year-old boy with an assault rifle and a uniform many sizes too big for me. I can still hear the voice of a gigantic Zulu I came to call my friend and brother as we spoke one night under a tree in the South African bush.

I can still smell and taste the air of Scotland, hear the incessant calls of the seagulls, and picture the glens and lochs of the Highlands—a place so beautiful that if it were a woman, men would write her poems of affection, bring her flowers, and fall at her feet. I can still see that black-haired girl from the youth hostel in a chair in front of the fireplace, reading the latest fashion magazine. I can still see the lights of Paris from the top of the Eiffel Tower. I remember the sounds and conversations, and as I look back on these mental images now, I can finally see how everything has invariably led me to this very moment.

The hopes and dreams of youth make us impervious to the consequence of time, but the reflection of time within our hearts is inescapable (some of us are old souls), and even though the exact moment of my first step on this journey is veiled by the silliness of youth, my heart points me to only one moment and place in time: an Air Force training facility nearly seventy miles north of Pretoria, South Africa.

Those that are most quiet have the most to say; I am one of those. Some people live on the outside while others live on the inside; I am one of those. A man who lives on the inside lives very close to his heart; I am one of those. If ever a description of such a man's journey in search of God is warranted, let mine be the one.

The fact is, lost sheep are found, some after a short time, while others stray so far they need passports to find their way back home. I was the kind of sheep that needed a passport. This is the story of three people who, unbeknownst to me at the time, guided me on this journey.

# 2

## CAMO CREAM

*Friendship is born at that moment when one person says to another: "What! You too? I thought I was the only one."*

—C. S. LEWIS

I can vividly remember the day I lost faith and trust in the church of my youth. When I was born in 1975 in South Africa, Apartheid was already a reality since 1948 and I didn't know what life before that was like.[1] It is not possible to compare an apple to an orange when you have never seen or tasted an orange before and when your knowledge about apples is very limited to begin with. There were no black people in my church. There were no black children in my school.

---

1 Apartheid (an Afrikaans word meaning "separateness") was a system of legal racial segregation enforced by the National Party government in South Africa between 1948 and 1994, under which the rights of the majority black inhabitants of South Africa were curtailed and minority rule by whites was maintained. Racial segregation in South Africa began in colonial times, but apartheid as an official policy was introduced after the general election of 1948. From 1958, Blacks were deprived of their citizenship, legally becoming citizens of one of ten tribally based self-governing homelands called Bantustans, four of which (Transkei, Ciskei, Venda, and Bophuthatswana) became nominally independent states. The government segregated education, medical care, and other public services, and provided black people with services inferior to those of whites.

My first recollection of the manifestation of racial segregation was during one summer vacation on the south coast of South Africa when I was very little (possibly even preschool, because I needed my dad's help to visit the bathroom). On our way to the public toilets on the beach, we passed a sign, and I remember asking my dad what the sign said. (I was beginning to read but still needed his help with some of the big words.) He read the sign for me, and it simply said, "Whites only." I asked him what it meant, and he told me that only white people were allowed on that particular beach. I didn't understand, but I remember thinking, *I'm glad I'm white.*

Growing up in South Africa in the late '70s and during the 1980s was very confusing to a young boy with an overactive imagination. Prime-time television news hinted at the fact that black people were an unruly bunch who liked to protest in the streets and burn things. Of course, I had no idea why they were protesting and burning things, and I never thought to ask why. I accepted it as a consequence of living in Africa; things were just the way they were because of my location on the planet. It had to be in black people's nature to want to burn things, throw stones, and protest in the streets, whereas white people liked to listen to music, watch rugby games, have barbeques and drink beer, and go to church on Sundays. Life was an apple, and the existence of an orange never occurred to me.

Like I said, I was a boy with an overactive imagination, and it was true paradise for such a boy to grow up in South Africa. My dad was the manager of a farm, and I was its king, and perhaps only a king can know the elation of ruling a vast empire (especially a ten-year-old king). O, the games I played!

During this time we were taught about Zulu history at school, and my imagination was set alight to burn brightly in the darkness of monotony. We learned about the battle of Isandlwana in January 1879, when two thousand British soldiers armed with Martini-Henry breech-loading rifles and artillery encountered a twenty-thousand-strong Zulu army of warriors armed with iron spears and cowhide shields. Being outnumbered ten to one, the British had no option but to be decimated. I remember many an afternoon after school reenacting that battle, attacking everything that looked even remotely British, including trash cans, trees, shrubs, and pets.

This time also coincided with a television drama about the life of King Shaka (the king of the Zulus) and his mother, Nandi, which further fueled my imagination and created even longer-lasting and more intensive battles. King Shaka revolutionized Zulu battle tactics by substituting the throwing spear, or *assegai*, for a shorter stabbing spear, seeing no sense in supplying their enemies with deadly projectiles that could be picked up and thrown back. As far as I was concerned, being a Zulu warrior was the epitome of manhood, and I was a magnificent Zulu warrior (and my dog was a magnificent British target). Such were the days of a young boy growing up in South Africa—an apple with no idea of the existence of an orange.

But I digress. It's time that I lose trust and faith in the church of my youth. When I grew up, terms like "the communist threat" and "the black threat" were used interchangeably (not by the church, but by people attending that church), and the first real contact I had with black people (other than the gardener or laborers) occurred when I joined the South African Air Force when I was eighteen years old.

Only a person who has served in the military knows what it feels like to step off the bus that very first day and have people shout at you from every direction for no apparent reason. But the volume of the shouting and the contents of the orders convince you that you must have done something wrong and that your inevitable punishment (perhaps even death) was only moments away.

The most common question among the men during the first few days was "What did we do wrong?" But after the first week we sort of figured out that the shouting means that you either have to look busy or do what the other guys are doing in a hurry. But even stranger than being shouted at for no apparent reason was the mysterious disappearance of friends that you made in the first few moments before "the haircut." People look entirely different with no hair on their heads, and after the haircut, you had to make friends all over again as a result of not being able to recognize your existing friends and remember their names.

There was no segregation in the military. White and black recruits slept together, ate together, and marched in formation together. We ran together, showered together, cleaned our rifles, and polished our boots together. And because of this proximity, many fights broke out. I remember one day when we were supposed to work in the garden (the drill sergeants called it base beautification), and a white guy and a black guy started fighting. I don't know what the fight was about, but I am convinced that they would have killed each other had we not intervened. They ran at each other, one armed with garden scissors and the other armed with a spade. Each was resolved to end the other's existence, and it took at least ten men to separate them. Many fights broke out in the first few weeks, most of which were between white and black recruits.

Although we shared everything and did everything together, there was a noticeable segregation when the drill sergeants were kind enough to give us water breaks. White recruits would coalesce into a single entity, and the black recruits would do the same. The white recruits would speak Afrikaans or English, and the black recruits would speak in their language. Although we wore the same uniforms, our similarities ended there. Drinking water became a time when white would stare at black and black would stare right back. The tension in those first few weeks was almost tangible.

Initially the tension was between white and black, but tension started to develop between fat and fit and between lazy and energetic. Punishment was never delivered on an individual basis but as a group. If one was late, all were late. If one failed a fitness test, all failed. The development of a group identity slowly emerged as a result, and that was when the fights ended. Water breaks were no longer a time for racial identification but a time for drinking water. Even the two who wanted to kill each other in the garden drank from the same water bottle. We became soldiers and brothers every time the drill sergeants gave us a few minutes to drink water.

During the last couple of weeks of training, we had to complete two weeks of field exercises. Now, the military has a very peculiar but necessary setup when it comes to field exercises; it's simply called the buddy system. Every recruit in the squadron had to buddy-up with another. This buddy was your lifeline during two weeks of hell on earth. He was the one who picked you up when you fell down. He was the one who ate with you, slept with you, and cleaned his rifle with you. Your buddy was your first and last hope of completing the field exercises in one piece, because during the last few days of training, live ammunition would be used.

But we weren't allowed to choose our own buddies that day. When we stepped off the bus at the training camp, the drill sergeants were ready with lists. They chose our buddies for us, and they found the pairs very amusing. Fat were paired with thin. Strong were paired with weak. Fast were paired with slow. I ended up with the biggest Zulu in the entire squadron. He was big, black, and frightening. "This is your buddy," they said. "Never leave his side. In fact, if he wants to pee, you hold it for him." None of us went that far.

One night, the platoons were assembled and given maps and grid references. Then we were instructed to march to the grid references and disappear. (I believe the purpose of this particular exercise was to test our knowledge of what we had learned about night camouflage.) Zulu and I paired up, got into platoon formation, and walked for what seemed like a thousand miles with backpacks weighing nearly sixty pounds.

Later that night, when we arrived at what we unanimously agreed to be the proper reference on the map, the platoon split up and the buddies got together. But Zulu and I didn't speak much. In fact, no one spoke much. It was April 1994, just a couple of days before the first democratic elections.[1] It was as if the entire country was gripped by nervous tension. Some people even stocked up on water and canned food, expecting that a bloody civil war would soon follow. That was why the white and black recruits didn't talk much. We wore the same uniforms, carried the same rifles, ate the same rations, but it was as if we were on opposite sides of an imminent battle. It was a very strange time to be in the military.

I hid my kit behind a tree and started to apply camo cream to my face and to the exposed parts of my arms, as the drill sergeants were going to try to find us later that night and we were threatened with "severe pain" if they succeeded.

---

[1] Nelson Mandela was an anti-apartheid activist and the leader of the African National Congress's armed wing Umkhonto we Sizwe (the Spear of the Nation). The South African courts had convicted him on charges of sabotage, as well as other crimes committed while he led the movement against apartheid. In accordance with his conviction, Mandela served twenty-seven years in prison, spending many of these years on Robben Island. Following his release from prison on February 11, 1990, Mandela supported reconciliation and negotiation, and helped lead the transition toward multiracial democracy in South Africa. He won the first democratic elections held on April 27, 1994.

After I had transformed myself into a veritable African bush, I walked over to Zulu, who didn't do much in the way of hiding himself or transforming into a piece of African flora. I took the camo cream from my pocket, handed it to him, and said, "Here, cover your face." Zulu looked at me as if I had just hatched from a gigantic egg that was laid only seconds before by a miniature pink elephant. "It's dark. I'm black," he said.

Zulu's point was made and taken. For just a moment the tension in that little part of South Africa was broken as we burst out laughing. "I'm what you people call non-reflective," he said. "You're the one who stands out like a full moon on a cloudless night, but that stuff on your face will work for tonight."

Some of the platoons were found, but our platoon remained undiscovered. It wasn't because we were masters of camouflage but, as it turned out, we weren't anywhere near the correct grid reference on the map. The drill sergeants called us countless times over the field radio with threats of "severe pain" if we didn't show ourselves, only to receive radio static as an answer. A quick platoon vote concluded that a good night's sleep was more important and that we would hunker down for the night and take our punishment in the morning. Zulu and I collected our sleeping bags and made ourselves comfortable under a tree.

"Do you think anything will happen?" I asked him after I was finally comfortable in my sleeping bag.

"They are going to drill us into the dust for sure, but that will only happen in the morning. Tonight we will hide like leopards, and tomorrow we will take our punishment like lions."

"I'm not talking about the drill sergeants. Do you think anything will happen after the elections?"

Zulu sat up and looked at the stars, and for a while I thought that he wasn't going to answer me. He looked down, took a handful of grass and soil, held it to his nose, inhaled, and said, "Jesus loves this country. Nothing will happen."

I don't think I can describe the effect Zulu's words had on me. I have certainly heard of black Christians before, but almost as a kind of phenomenon—and certainly not of a Zulu who believed in Jesus. There were no black people in my church. There were no black children in my school. Never before that moment had I heard a black man, other than Bishop Desmond Tutu, speak of Jesus. "Jesus loves this country,"

Zulu had said. "Nothing will happen." I believed him. I felt safe that night, sleeping next to a gigantic Zulu who had no fear for South Africa's future. And even though our punishment was extremely severe the next morning, nothing could nullify the peace I felt. My faith and trust in the church of my youth died that day, somewhere under a tree in the South African bush. The elections came and went. There was no civil war. Nothing happened.

I learned many valuable lessons during those two weeks of hell on earth. First, do not get too close to the guys who smoke weed on a regular basis when the exercise is with live ammunition, as they are the ones who are most likely to kill themselves accidentally or shoot their friends. Second, when you put white and black people in a situation where they are equally ill-treated—where their suffering is equally as bad—skin color disappears completely.

Zulu and I became close friends and remained in contact with each other for seven years.

# 3

# Naked and Dead

*Death is not the greatest loss in life. The greatest loss is what dies inside us while we live.*

—NORMAN COUSINS

Zulu's words had a profound effect on me, and in many ways that night under the tree with him served as a catalyst and set a journey in motion that would last many years. I began to realize that the "apple" of my life was an immense lie, or at least a colossal misconception. After the elation of President Nelson Mandela's landslide political victory in April 1994 quieted down, the Truth and Reconciliation Commission began the painful task of mending the hearts of South Africans.[1] It was only then that many learned about killings, disappearances, and tortures for the first time, and as many others, I hated seeing those mothers and fathers on television cry for justice. I hated seeing the perpetrators begging for forgiveness (some sincerely and others less so). I hated the descriptions of how some were tortured, killed, and unceremoniously disposed of simply because they didn't agree with the government's policies.

---

1 The Truth and Reconciliation Commission was a court-like body assembled in South Africa after the abolition of apartheid. Witnesses who were identified as victims of gross human rights violations were invited to give statements about their experiences, and some were selected for public hearings and broadcast on television. Perpetrators of violence could also give testimony and request amnesty from both civil and criminal prosecution.

My life was an apple and the existence of an orange became painfully clear, and I remember experiencing immense guilt (like many white South Africans did). Even though Apartheid wasn't my or the church's doing, those atrocities happened under a so-called Christian government, and as a result, I began to examine myself and my religious beliefs with a microscope. I realized that I was never really a Christian. It is not possible to call yourself a Christian just because you come from a Christian home and attended Sunday school. No, the ingredients of Christianity are not restricted to the ones that are close at hand or easily obtained, but encompass a full range of human emotions and virtues that are measured, added, deleted, weighed, and mixed with a vital source, without which the end product will not even come close to resembling what Christianity is actually about. I was never a Christian. Not even close.

When I was little, Jesus and Santa Claus were the same person. For me, praying was a lot like going through a mental gift list, and although Santa Claus disappeared as I grew older, Jesus never lost the "bearer of gifts" image. I went to church and attended Sunday school every Sunday, but for me it was only a habit and a ritual. It was something our family did every Sunday. It didn't require thought. It didn't require mental commitment. The only requirement was attendance. For me, Sunday was just a barrier between Saturday and Monday.

Since Zulu and I had met three years earlier, I began to doubt—the kind of doubt that feels like it has always been there under the surface, waiting for the right time to emerge so that it can make you feel lost and adrift. Whenever I went to church, I felt removed and isolated. And I didn't feel an emotional connection with what was said or with the other people in church. It was easy to notice that many other people in church felt a real connection and perhaps even had a personal relationship with God, something that was acutely missing in my life. I began to feel that I simply didn't fit the profile. Being in church doesn't make you a Christian, just as being on a launch pad doesn't make you a rocket.

I began to ask, "What good is Christianity? I can lead a fulfilling life and be a good man without being a Christian." As far as I was concerned, Christianity was comprised of people, and people are so easily misled. I simply wasn't moved, and I'm the kind of man that has to be moved in order to get any kind of response or reaction. I didn't experience any sort of emotion in church—or with Christianity, for that matter—except perhaps guilt over not experiencing a spiritual connection. I wasn't moved by the Bible; I wasn't moved by the church; and I didn't feel moved by God.

Most of us have events in our lives we find uncomfortable to think about; these events usually include moments we didn't expect at the time and never thought possible. For me, this event was when my father began to show signs of a disease when I was about twelve years old (which was also around the time I stopped imagining that I was a Zulu warrior). It was hard as a young boy to notice the change in his demeanor and his personality: a force to be reckoned with on the farm was reduced to something other than forceful. He was diagnosed with bipolar disorder—a chemical imbalance in the brain—and admitted to a state mental hospital for a time. I have no idea what they did to him in that hospital or what his treatment involved, but I had heard rumors of electroshock therapy (applying low-level electric shocks to the brain to restore the chemical balance). My father was never the same.

My parents divorced when I was fourteen years old, and like many teenagers who experience a divorce, I found an emotional escape. Some find that escape in friends or sport. Others find it in cigarettes or recreational drugs. I found an escape in books, but more about my literary retreat later.

My mother remarried, and I suddenly found myself in a new family with new brothers and a sister. I had a new home and a new life, but the memory of my father never left me alone. I knew him for only twelve years, and then he disappeared into the gray area of his emotions and moods. I wanted to know him, but as he was found unfit to care for children, I could visit him only on weekends, and I soon grew to hate those visits. It was like spending time with a stranger that only looked a lot like my father.

We tried to build a model airplane together but the medication he had to take made his hands shake. It was hard to see the disappointment and frustration in his eyes as he stuck the wings on crooked or accidentally punched a hole in the delicate paper covering the balsawood frame. He even cried once, and I pretended that I needed to go to the bathroom so that he could cry in peace and without shame. I was never more relieved than when the model was finally finished, and I always had an excuse for not visiting on the weekends that followed. The guilt I felt over not wanting to visit him was overwhelming. Isn't it strange how we feel more perplexed about withholding love than about harboring hate?

After I joined the Air Force and after completing most of my training, I decided to move in with my father in an effort to reconnect with him and to get to know him. I was twenty years old then and felt that I had grown emotionally stronger than the fourteen-year-old boy who used to spend time with him on Saturdays. But being emotionally strong is particularly hard when you are emotionally involved. I was his son; he was my father.

Our domestic arrangements and routine depended wholly on his moods. There were days when he was upbeat, funny, and energetic. He would play his favorite CD and whistle the tune while watering the garden or doing some other chore. Those days were the good days, the days when he left like a father and companion. But those days were few and far between. The bad days were more regular.

I worked at Air Force headquarters at the time and was always the first to get up in the morning and make breakfast. If he wasn't downstairs in thirty minutes, I knew it would be a bad day. On these days he would be short-tempered, grouchy, and unpredictable. I tried my best to stay out of his way when he was like that, but sometimes he would yell and fight with me over small things. I always apologized, because I knew he didn't mean it.

And then there were the sad days—days when he would cry for no apparent reason. To me, those days were the worst, because he would drink more than usual. I hid most of the alcohol in the house, but I always kept a bottle in plain sight in the kitchen. I know it sounds strange, but I felt that he earned it; he hadn't chosen to have a chemically imbalanced brain.

A sad day would be followed by a confused day. Because he took his medication and drank alcohol on sad days, it made him terribly confused and hard to understand the following day. I was in the kitchen one morning preparing breakfast when my father came downstairs, walked into the kitchen in his underwear, lifted the lid on the kitchen garbage bin, and urinated into it. I was stunned. After he was done, he carefully closed the lid again and turned to leave, but as reality suddenly dawned on him, he turned to me and casually said, "I just p*ssed in the garbage bin, didn't I?" I was late for work that day, as my father and I couldn't stop laughing for nearly an hour.

I soon figured out that I had a secret weapon in the form of ice cream. Whether it was a good, bad, or sad day, a bowl of chocolate ice cream seemed to reach him on a level nothing and no one else could. Even when I was out with friends or doing what twenty-somethings do, I would get a text or voice message on my phone every once in a while asking me to have a bowl of ice cream with him.

Two years later, my father moved into a smaller apartment, and I found a room in a boarding house closer to Air Force headquarters. I was scheduled to complete an officer's formative course in September 1997, after which I would become a junior officer. But even though I didn't live with my father anymore, I still visited him regularly.

I was with my girlfriend one night when I received another voice message from him. He had bought ice cream and wanted to know if I would spend some time with him, as he was having a "sad day" (we had adopted a "good, bad, sad" system shortly after I moved in with him). But I was with my girlfriend and decided to ignore his message.

The following afternoon I was at my mother's house when my older brother called. "I think Dad is dying" was all he said. I drove over to his place like a maniac and as I walked into my father's bedroom, my brother said, "Neil, Dad is dead."

Many things died that day. No young man should see his own father dead and naked and say to himself, "This is my fault." No young man should look on his father's lifeless face and think, "This could have been prevented with a simple bowl of ice cream." He had taken a handful of pills the previous night and gone to bed. He never woke up. It was a Tuesday—twenty-two days after my twenty-second birthday. Why would God let someone live a life of unhappiness only to die naked and alone? What good is Christianity? What good is God? Many things died with my father, including my religion, and after my father's funeral, I broke up with my girlfriend as well.

# 4

# I Kneel in Adoration

*I love you without knowing how, or when, or from where. I love you straightforwardly, without complexities or pride; so I love you because I know no other way.*

—PABLO NERUDA

*(100 Love Sonnets)*

After successfully completing the officer formative course that I mentioned in the previous chapter, I was selected to attend the military academy. In fact, my successful completion of officer training was required, as only officers can attend the academy. At any rate, I went to the military academy on the west coast of South Africa in 1998, when I was twenty-two years old.

I was young and restless and eager to learn. I was arrogant and presumptuous and convinced that I held the world in the palm of my hand. Yet I have always felt separated from this world in a certain sense. Sometimes I felt like an observer looking in from the outside, and because of this I have always kept to myself in a certain way: I have lived most of my life on the inside. When I was little, I could play alone for hours (as a Zulu warrior). Even though I didn't spend as much time tilting at windmills as I grew older, I still had a very active imagination. It would prove to be my greatest enemy as I believed without a doubt that I was my father's killer. But let's leave this issue here for the time being.

I remember the first time I read something that moved me in the true emotional sense of the word. I was sixteen years old when I got ahold of my mother's copy of *The Treasured Writings of Khalil Gibran.* I paged through the book one idle afternoon and came upon a chapter titled *The Broken Wings.* The story tells of a young Lebanese man who fell in love with the daughter of a friend of his father. Her name was Selma Karamy, and she fell in love with him too. But the cruelty of the real world soon stepped in as she was to be married to a bishop's nephew—a man she didn't love.

Their story tore at my heart. Every sentence of Gibran's flowery language made me feel their pain and sorrow. Later, after she was married to the bishop's nephew, they still met once a month at a secluded temple, but never once broke the vows a married woman makes to her husband. The love they had for each other was pure and utter torture.

Selma had children by the bishop's nephew, but her love for a certain young man did not waiver, and she instinctively knew what had to be done: she had to sacrifice herself, her dreams, and her love so that he may live. Their last meeting in that temple tormented me the most. She spoke to him with words I had never heard before. She spoke from a place that had only love, saying, "The hour of separation has come." She would not meet him again for fear of what the bishop's nephew might to do him. She set him free and returned to a loveless live.

I was amazed with her act and even more amazed with how Gibran described it:

> Many a time, since that night, I have thought of the spiritual law which made Selma prefer death to life, and many a time I have made a comparison between nobility of sacrifice and happiness of rebellion to find out which one is nobler and more beautiful; but until now I have distilled only one truth out of the whole matter, and this truth is sincerity, which makes all our deeds beautiful and honorable. And this sincerity was in Selma Karamy.

Sincerity was beautiful to me. Of all the human virtues, sincerity was the noblest. Even at sixteen years of age, I could not deny the logic of a Lebanese man I had never met. In my heart of hearts, I hoped that his words were true: "In every young man's life there is a 'Selma' who appears to him suddenly while in the spring of life and transforms his solitude into happy moments and fills the silence of his nights with music."

I became a romantic when I read that book, or rather, I discovered that I was one all along.

My love for books was instilled in me by a mother, who took me to the library every week, even before I could read. Initially, I was drawn to books with pictures in them, as they made more sense to me than words, but as I grew older, I was drawn to books with words that were as beautiful as pictures. After reading Khalil Gibran, I began to read as much as I could. I fell in love with the classics and even ventured into poetry. Even today, the mention of names such as Gibran, Shakespeare, Milton, Yeats, Blake, Homer, Lawrence, Neruda, and so on evoke feelings I can describe only as a feeling of belonging.

My first attempt at writing poetry was dismal to say the least, but like so many poets and writers, I believed that my best poem or best story was the one I hadn't written yet. However, attempting to write the poem or story I hadn't written yet only revealed to me that I did not write the one I hadn't written yet, but something else. Regardless of my many failures, poetry came from a place inside me that had no fear of failure or ridicule. It dripped from my hands like the slow ooze of honey. Even after my father (and my religion) died, poetry never left me. It was as constant as the motion of our planet.

And so I arrived at the military academy: a fatherless, romantic, nonreligious, imaginative man obsessed with sincerity that lived on the inside.

In general, all the students at the military academy are officers, but the Air Force, being the superior arm of service of the South African National Defence Force (let no one tell you otherwise), sees it fit only to bestow a commission after the individual has proven himself. First-year Air Force students remain candidate officers until they have successfully completed their first year of study. A candidate officer (or CO) isn't really a rank, but more like a situation—the lowest form of primordial life imaginable—which meant that I had to salute practically everything with a heartbeat.

But this fact didn't hamper my spirit too much. I had always thought of myself as a lone ranger—an independent and mysterious man; a man of action rather than words; a man with a commanding presence; a man who would disappear into the sunset on a horse at the end of the day; a man with a desperate need to become an officer.

The first few weeks were demanding to say the least. I had six subjects with lecturers who never quite understood the fact that a first-year student needs to sleep from time to time. We were covered with work and assignments, and every now and then we were surprised with a class test most probably compiled with the sole purpose of making us feel that whatever we did wasn't enough. But for some reason I found studying very easy, as it was like reading. It made more sense to me to understand rather than to learn, and like many people with this ability, I found a reason to be lazy. I was not lazy in a military sense (heaven forbid), but lazy in the sense that I saw no need to take notes in class. I had textbooks; books were meant to be read; and reading was something I was very good at. Seeing that I didn't spend as much time studying as some of the other students did, I had time on my hands for other things.

Cicero, a Roman philosopher, statesman, lawyer, orator, and political theorist said, "To know nothing about before you were born is to remain forever a child." I didn't want to remain a child. I didn't want to remain an eighteen-year-old under a tree with a Zulu. I wanted to know everything about before I was born. I was required to read textbooks about political science, military geography, military strategy, psychology, and computer programing languages, but I also delved into the world of history, philosophy, evolution, and science, hoping to find the true identity of God in some obscure place. I wanted to create a mental map of some sort—something I could follow with logic. But first, I fell in love.

One day during teatime (a remnant of British rule), I was standing alone and smoking a cigarette (as is only fitting for a candidate officer to do—not the smoking but the separation). I was thinking about the Lone Ranger again and how wonderful it would be to ride off into the sunset at the end of that day. My mind was filled with thoughts of freedom and mystery, of gunfights (with fellow students that I didn't particularly care for), and of horses. And that was when I saw her. I had seen her a few times before but had never really looked at her until that day. My eyes were fixed on her as she stirred her tea, and everything around me became quiet. I was like a statue for what seemed like an eternity. Suddenly I pictured my imaginary horse running over the hills with no rider on its back. Without hesitation (and without me even knowing it),

I had dismounted my horse and set it free to graze in the pasture. After all, who needs a horse? Who needs a life of sweat and dust? The sun had to set without me that day. You see, the unthinkable had happened: the Lone Ranger had fallen in love.

She was in the navy, and I found her insanely beautiful. She moved like a jungle cat and had bumps and dents in all the right places. To look at her took my breath away. There were only two problems though: she was an officer and I was a CO. She was a second-year student and I was a first-year. I had a bigger chance of setting foot on the moon than I had to even speak to her.

No one could ever know about my feelings for her. I had to keep them secret. I had to approach her in a way that would keep my identity a secret. I did the only thing that came to mind, the only thing that made sense: I wrote a poem.

**I KNEEL IN ADORATION**

What if I could touch your face
or even keep your heart, and mind, and soul
in my left-hand pocket?
Then I would be a man,
dancing on the edge of ecstasy
waiting to explode
into a myriad of kaleidoscopic fantasies.

And it is not the tinge of morning's luster
or the enigmatic sparkle in your eyes
that makes me kneel in adoration.
No. Oh a thousand times no!
I swear it is the envy of the stars
and their endless lamentations
that bring tears to my sore eyes.

The next day, I put the poem in an envelope and wrote her name on the front, and even though I had no idea what I was going to do with it, I knew that a plan would develop as the day went by. After considering many options, I eventually decided to put the envelope in her mailbox (anonymously, of course). The idea was that she would find it and read it, and secretly I would be absolved of my sins (my sin being that I was a junior in rank, or rather, that I suffered from the complete absence of rank).

The following day, walking from one class to the next, I decided to see if there were any messages in "the Book." (This book was placed in a central location in the faculty building and used by anyone who wanted to leave a message for another. Lecturers usually left messages in the Book for students to inform them if class had been canceled, so it was usually the first stop for the day.) I paged through the book and found the following message: "To the one who wrote the poem: You made my day. Thanx."

I became a statue again. My heart beat faster than a freight train, and my mouth was suddenly dry. My senses were dull, and the only things that existed in those short seconds were that page in the Book and me. I felt like a king and the ruler of the universe.

That night I wrote some more poems, and they too mysteriously found their way into her mailbox. Every day she found a new poem, and every day I felt like a king. Although she still didn't know who I was, I didn't care. All I cared for was that she had a secret and that I knew what it was.

My anonymous poetic rendezvous with the navy girl lasted a few weeks—until the day my identity was discovered. I was minding my own business during teatime when she casually walked up to me and said, "Why don't you just tell me?" Various melodramatic thoughts flashed through my mind, all of which convinced me that I was a going to be a dead man before sunset. How had she known it was me? Somebody must have tipped her off! I couldn't speak. I just looked at her with confusion. She smiled, turned around, and walked away. Her smile burned through me like a raging fire. Again I became a statue.

I went to her dorm room that night to try to convince her that I was in fact able to speak and that being a statue was something I only did for fun. I cannot recall exactly how that night played out. I only know that it was wonderful being in her company. For some reason she found me very funny, and I loved the sound of her laughter; it made me feel warm in the center of my chest.

But my happiness was short-lived, as it turned out she had someone else on her mind. He was a final-year student and a captain in the army. He was older than I was, he was taller than I was, and he was my superior in rank. It is not easy being the Lone Ranger and disappearing into the sunset without an imaginary horse. The poems stopped, and I was relegated to a life on foot.

I spent the rest of the first and second semester doing what is expected from a first-year Air Force Intelligence student. My days were filled with thoughts about how a particular captain in the army would beg me for his life after I had driven over him with a steamroller. My favorite thought was how I would ignore his feeble screams as I put the steamroller into reverse to drive over him again.

Eventually the year came to an end and the academic recess arrived. I went home that year with one thing in mind: finding a new imaginary horse, one that wouldn't run off into the distance because of a mere woman. I was determined not to dismount ever again.

In January 1999, I was promoted to the rank of second lieutenant, and my days of being a candidate officer (the very lowest form of life) became a faint and distant memory. My mortal enemy (the captain) had obtained his degree the previous year, which meant he was no longer at the academy. That thought had not occurred to me, and I remember feeling utterly happy not to see him during the first morning parade of the first semester. I forgave him all his sins and decided not to kill him in his sleep after all. Everything was coming up roses. I was finally an officer; my new imaginary horse seemed to be very loyal and trustworthy; and my grave enemy (the captain) had left the battlefield.

The young lady, whom I'll call Navy, became my only thought, and I pursued her relentlessly for weeks. I am not sure if she fell in love or merely gave in, but very soon after I consciously decided to shoot my new imaginary horse with an imaginary gun (despite his loyalty and trustworthiness), Navy and I became friends. In many ways, she became my new religion. As I learned more about her, she became less like a goddess and more like a woman. It felt as if I had discovered paradise after a long and arduous journey. Getting to know her was like being lost in a wonderful garden, like being a pilgrim in a new and unknown land of terrible beauty.

**A PILGRIM'S WISH**

Incandescent in my nature
and secluded by my choice,
to be a mere observer
as she binds my heart forever.

To be close to such contentment
was never my intention,
but awesome is the journey
that she wills for me to take.

So I went without much protest
to this land that she has willed,
and I find myself a pilgrim
in the kingdom of her soul.

My heart is leaping lightly
as I trample on my way,
not man, nor beast, nor burden
shall be taking me away.

As the first week of our newfound friendship went slowly by, it dawned on me that something had to be done. After staring at myself in the mirror for an inordinate amount of time, a voice inside my head gave me no option but to listen: "Kiss her, you fool!" It was certainly not the first time that the thought of kissing her had entered my mind. In fact, I had wanted to kiss her that very first day when she held a teacup in her hands, but I think tackling her right there and then would have been viewed as assaulting a superior officer and landed me in the brig. I will not describe the details of that first kiss, but it is safe to say that following the night of the kiss, Navy and I became inseparable (and we kissed frequently).

Life became very different for me then. I was probably the only Air Force student on campus who knew something about ship stability and hull displacement, just because I spent time casually flipping through her textbooks. No longer did I feel the sting of my experiences and memories. Every minute spent with Navy felt like a reprieve from a sentence passed down from some unknown authority that cared nothing for my dreams, fantasies, and vulnerabilities.

The way she walked and carried herself, the sound of her laughter, and her tiniest gestures and features became ingrained in my conscious and unconscious mind. After a while I was even able to recognize her footsteps in the corridor of my dorm when she came walking to my room. There was nothing about her that I could not describe. Her smell, for instance, drove me crazy. At times she smelled like an ethereal combination of lavender and the color pink, and other times she smelled like a softer hue of yellow and citrus. When we fell asleep together, I would breathe her in as deep as I could until my lungs hurt from the exertion. She seeped through my cracks and became a vital part of me before I could spell the word *perfection.* I truly believed that if atoms can fuse to form new elements, so can hearts. Hearts fuse to form the exotic elements of contentment and bliss.

I like to recall one night in particular often with fondness. It was the night of a yearly event during which students and faculty members treated each other to cultured and tasteful entertainment and performances (the proceeds of ticket sales were usually donated to a local charity). It was a formal function, which meant that the men had to wear their military dress uniforms (which entailed the polishing and shining of buttons, epaulets, and shoes to the point of nausea), but the women only had to spend hideous amounts of money to buy new evening dresses for the occasion.

That night, the insignia of my rank, the buttons on my tunic, and every other piece of brass scattered across my uniform were polished to the brilliance of a cosmic body. My shoes were shined to a mirror finish, and I used three brand-new razor blades to achieve the smoothest shave in the history of man, after which I applied just the right amount of aftershave lotion. But the excitement that was slowly churning to full-blown hurricane status inside my chest had nothing to do with my meticulous preparation for a long-awaited event. No, Navy was going to be my companion, and I would happily have made the same effort even if it meant that she and I were only going to watch paint dry.

She didn't move that night like the other women did; she floated on a cushion of air. There was a particular sparkle in her eyes and the knowledge that it was just for me made me delirious with happiness. I was unable to distinguish myself from her that night. I was unable to tell where she began and where I stopped. I loved her so completely that even her imperfections became so beautiful that they touched me more deeply than the dawning of a perfect morning. Navy was like a rose, and although a rose has thorns, the fragrance made the occasional blood on my hands acceptable. I loved her more than I loved myself. We were best friends. She was my touchstone. I could go on to say that she talked like Marlene Dietrich, that she danced like Zizi Jeanmaire, that her clothes were all made by Balmain, and that there were diamonds and pearls in her hair, but none of this would be true. What I loved most about her is that she made me forget about chocolate ice cream, a tragic death, and an unnecessary funeral. All thoughts of God, religion, death, pain, and guilt fell away into nothingness.

# 5

# WITHER MY HEART

*I stood still, vision blurring, and in that moment, I heard my heart break. It was a small, clean sound, like the snapping of a flower's stem.*

—DIANA GABALDON

*(Dragonfly in Amber)*

In the middle of every academic year was a recess period of two months during which students could elect to complete training required by their respective arms of service and their particular fields of duty. Some students chose this period for training, while others were transferred to military bases across the country for a period of detached duty. Academic recess was usually welcomed by all, because it meant a much-needed change of scenery and a chance to get away from books and studying for a while. But I dreaded the arrival of the academic recess, because it meant that I had to go to an Air Force base in Pretoria and Navy had to report for naval combat officer training in Simonstown. I had a heavy heart the day I had to kiss her good-bye, because I wouldn't be able to see her for eight weeks. It was a bitter pill to swallow. I left the military academy for Pretoria with thoughts of her filling my mind.

Air Force Base Waterkloof (where I had to perform my detached duty for the recess period) looked nothing like the west coast I had grown to love so much. I couldn't see a beach from my office window, and there were no seagulls gliding on the breeze. But the presence of Navy was the one thing I missed the most: her smile, her bright eyes, and her laughter. I missed her like a vital organ.

**WITHER MY HEART**

Wither my heart! This cannot be true!
For the immense distance
has left me with an ache so deep
that I fear for my very life.

Wither my heart! This cannot be true!
That you are not within my reach,
and I must be content to fall asleep alone
in a bed that is not mine.

Wither my heart! This cannot be true!
On either side of the world
that two lovers should be apart
when it is frightfully winter.

After four weeks of absence I just couldn't stand it anymore, and I did what any normal man in love would do: I devised a plan to visit Navy for a week. After listening to my rational argument for nearly fifteen minutes, the commanding officer of 60 Squadron agreed to let me have a seat on the next Air Force Boeing 707 headed for Air Force Base Ysterplaat in Cape Town. Flying to Cape Town that day was a lot like flying into a dream, and I believe my longing to see her again made us fly that much faster. It had never occurred to me that in only four weeks of being apart, Navy's feelings for me could change.

I listened to her as she casually explained that she had found someone else, and in that instant something inside me shuddered to a standstill. Perhaps happiness in love moves inside us like the tides of the ocean, and perhaps that is what shuddered to a standstill inside me. These tides wash over us in slow, fluid movements, and over time we take their motion for granted. We take for granted that when the tide is at its lowest, it will build up again to achieve a high tide, but we so often forget that the tides of the ocean are a result of the moon's gravitational influence. Navy was my moon, and the tide of my happiness was suspended somewhere between high and low. My waters would become stagnant.

She agreed to let me use her car so I could drive back to Air Force Base Ysterplaat and get a room in the officers' mess for three days, after which she would pick up her keys from the mess office and drive it back to Simonstown.

Usually a body of water takes a good while to become stagnant, but in my case it was instantaneous. To be fair to Navy, the heartbreak that I experienced was totally exaggerated. She was by no means my first girlfriend, but she was the first to cover me completely in the cloak of infatuation, and to be covered in that cloak was also to be shielded from pain—a pain that now had no barrier between me and it.

### I DRIVE . . .

I drive around in Cape Town a lot,
aimlessly,
but it is her car and her keys
and her Tori Amos
playing on the radio.

I want to delete myself;
I want to delete her face
and her voice from my mind,
but I know that I will only
hate myself afterward.

I saw the same movie
for the second time today,
but still didn't quite get the plot.
Afterward I walked around in a bookshop
for a while
and eventually bought one
containing poems of a Chilean author.
I drank coffee—
the filtered type;
and as soon as her memory
crept back into my mind

I ran off without paying,
got back into her car
and drove away
with an inexplicable urge
to leave Tori Amos
bleeding in the parking lot.

My return flight was on a Wednesday morning, and as I looked at Table Mountain through the window as we gained altitude through the clouds, I think I went a little insane.

There were three weeks left of the academic recess, but this time I didn't hatch a grand scheme to find an imaginary horse or anything ridiculous like that. Instead I did nothing apart from going to work, writing reports, spending time with family and friends, and avoiding my thoughts.

**UNTITLED**

I woke up
but went nowhere.
I drew a warm bath
but didn't get in.
I cooked dinner
but didn't eat.
I went to bed again
but couldn't sleep.

Most of the time I miss her—
sometimes.

I listen—
but her voice has died.
I look—
but her image no longer comes to me.
I reach out—
but my hands will no longer follow her lines
or touch her skin.
My arms will no longer pull her close to me,

and my lips will no longer graze upon hers.

Sometimes I miss her—
most of the time.

Though I can never forget
this is the last poem
that I will write in her name,
and with its end
I believe will end my pain.

But my pain was far from over. I had to return to the military academy and face her. I had to face all those memories and all those places. I had to face the stars and the moon and the beach, and I had to face the painful reality that even though it had been more than a year since my father took his own life, I had never grieved over it. I had avoided that grief for a very long time and had even managed to forget about it for a while by creating an impossible image and fantasy of falling in love and being in love. But now there would be no more forgetting, and I knew that remembering would return with a vengeance.

The second semester of that year started with one student less, as I was not entirely present. Seeing Navy only twisted the dagger that was already lodged firmly in my heart. To see her with other men was to remove that dagger and replace it with sufficient force so as to ensure a new sensation of pain, much worse than the pain I had grown used to. The sadness and pain gave way to anger, and that's when the darkness came. It was a darkness that would change me in every possible way; a darkness that would stay with me for a very, very long time; a darkness that would eventually force me to the Highlands of Scotland.

I still felt responsible for my father's death, and along with the guilt that had already made itself at home in my heart, I had to accommodate an entirely different yet no less destructive feeling: inadequacy. For the second time I experienced the death of a religion; granted it was a false one, but for the first time I experienced the anguish of it. If I was quiet before, I became even quieter then. If I had a secret and separate life before, I became even more secretive and secluded then.

# 6

# MERMAID

*Science without religion is lame,*
*religion without science is blind.*

—ALBERT EINSTEIN

Before I left for the military academy, Zulu and I agreed to call each other regularly. Most of our conversations were about what we were up to and what things had changed in our lives since the last time we spoke. He was proud of me the day I told him that I was going to become an officer. He would remain an enlisted man, as he never finished high school, and for some reason he felt that becoming officer in the military was a monumental accomplishment. When I told him that I was selected to attend the military academy, I could feel his beaming smile through the telephone.

I never quite understood why Zulu was so proud of me. It was almost as if my success instantly belonged to him too. Perhaps our friendship made it possible for him to imagine a life where he actually finished high school and didn't grow up poor. Our friendship made Zulu believe that life was fair and that bad things never happened to good people. He was the only one of my friends who knew the truth behind my father's death, and he was the only one I trusted with it.

I had always wanted to ask Zulu something, but in many ways I was afraid of what he would say. Perhaps it was the guilt I carried with me as a white man that made me fear his response, but he always had a way of cutting through all ambiguity and guile and letting me be who I am without fear. It was a question I simply had to ask: "Do you ever get angry?" So I asked one day during one of our many telephone conversations.

"About what?"

"Well, about Apartheid."

Zulu was quiet for a moment. "Yes, I do get angry sometimes. I remember being very angry when Hector Pieterson was killed during the Soweto uprising.[1] I was very young at the time, but his death made me angry, mostly because my father was very angry. Many awful things happened in those days." Zulu sighed before he continued. "I am not a kafir, Neil."[2] He said it without warning, and the word startled me. It was almost as if it didn't belong in his mouth. I tried to picture him at the other end of the line, speaking that word into his cell phone. How many times before had I used that word in my lifetime as a joke or in anger?

But now I was friends with a Zulu, and the word stung me like it never had before. "Did you know that the word is actually Arabic in origin and that it means 'unbeliever'?" he asked. "I still get called a kafir sometimes, but when it happens, I just smile, knowing that they are actually referring to themselves. Listen, Neil, Apartheid is a thing of

---

1 The Soweto uprising, or Soweto riots, was a series of clashes in Soweto, South Africa, on June 16, 1976, between black youths and the South African authorities. The riots grew out of protests against the policies of the National Party government and its apartheid regime. Hector Pieterson (1964-June 16, 1976) became the iconic image of the 1976 Soweto uprising in apartheid South Africa when a news photograph by Sam Nzima of the dying Hector being carried by a fellow student was published around the world. He was killed at the age of twelve when the police opened fire on protesting students.

2 Sometimes spelled *kaffer* or *kafir*. Generally considered a racial or ethnic slur in modern usage, it was previously a neutral term for black southern African people. The original meaning of the word is "heathen," "unbeliever," or "infidel," from the Arabic *kafir*, and is still being used with this meaning by Muslims. In South Africa today, the term is used both as an insult and as a common word for a black person. In any case, the term is regarded by most as highly offensive (in the same way as *nigger* in other countries).

the past. We should focus on the future. I think South Africans should develop a sense of humor. Do you remember that night when you handed me the camo cream? Now, that was funny, wasn't it?"

"Yes it was." I chuckled.

"Europeans brought many things to this country, and if I ignore the oppression for just a moment, they also brought Christianity with them. I will endure a thousand oppressive regimes if it means that only one of them introduces me to the God I know today."

Zulu always found a way of bringing God into any conversation.

Not wanting to go through the anguish of bumping into Navy in the faculty building when moving from one class to the next, I decided to make a slight adjustment to my sleeping pattern. I stayed awake at night and asked all the questions one could possibly ask about religion and God: Does God exist? If so, who is he? Did Jesus really exist? Can I believe the Gospels? What is the origin of morality? What is the origin of everything? Am I a deist or a theist? Am I a creationist or an evolutionist? Why are religions so exclusive? What about other religions? Does my life have a purpose? Do I have any intrinsic value?

My many conversations with Zulu prompted me finally to begin a quest that was long overdue, and the situation with Navy gave me an excuse to remove myself completely from academy life and enter a world where nothing existed but my thoughts and questions. I skipped classes and did my own thing in my own time.

On the cover of the December 1969 issue of *National Geographic Magazine* was a picture of an astronaut standing on the moon. I remember being fascinated by that picture when I was very little. A man was standing on the moon! Like a typical young boy who grew up watching episodes of *Buck Rogers,* I wanted to become an astronaut (until I found out that South Africa didn't have a space program). Since then I had always been fascinated with space, and now I had the time to find out how it all happened and where everything had come from.

Before the 1920s, scientists believed that the universe was static and eternal. Then a brilliant astronomer named Edwin Hubble determined that all the things in the universe are moving away from each other. This discovery would have far-reaching implications and would forever change our knowledge about the universe. If things are moving away from each other, then as you go back in time, things must have been closer together, until you reach a point in the distant past (roughly 13.7 billion years ago) when everything came together at one single point—a point called a singularity. This singularity created everything out of seemingly nothing—every star, every planet, every atom, every man, woman and child—a result of a single defining moment in time called the Big Bang.

But why did it bang? How did it bang? What was there before the bang? These are all questions that are extremely hard to answer, but I made it my mission to answer them for myself in a satisfactory manner. Since I had decided to model my sleeping pattern after that of a vampire (asleep during the day and awake at night), I had more than enough time to read and investigate by ordering books from Cape Town and reading articles on the internet. I would have the origin of the universe figured out in no time, or so I thought. I wanted to create a quick and simple rundown of what happened that I could understand.

It seems that the universe sprang into existence from nothing—one moment nothing, and the next moment, well, everything. In that instant of creation, all the laws of physics began to take shape, and the first force to emerge was gravity. Gravity plays a vital role in the formation of the universe: too little gravity and the universe fails; too much gravity and the universe collapses into black holes. But, lucky for us, our universe began with a Goldilocks value of gravity: just right.

The universe expands in every direction at incredible speed. Scientists believe it took less than a millionth of a millionth of a millionth of a millionth of a second for the universe to expand from the size of an atom to the size of a baseball; it was expanding faster than the speed of light. This early universe was still just a ball of super-heated energy, and it was not possible for matter to exist. It was simply too hot for atoms to exist. But as the universe cooled, energy was converted into subatomic particles that popped in and out of existence, but these particles were too unstable to produce the universe as we know it today. As the universe cooled, however, the particles stopped changing back into energy.

Then the universe entered a critical stage: matter and antimatter collisions. When matter and antimatter come into contact, they annihilate each other. As we know, everything in the universe is made of matter—from you to your dog to your toothbrush. If there were equal amounts of matter and antimatter, the universe would have no matter; but lucky for us, there was just a little more matter than antimatter.

The universe was still less than one second old, and no atoms existed yet. As the universe cooled down even more, it became possible for atoms to exist, and the first element that took shape was hydrogen.

In only three minutes, the universe expanded from infinitely small to light-years in size. It took another 380,000 years for the universe to cool down so that electrons could stick to atoms to enable the mass production of hydrogen, helium, and lithium.

Clouds of hydrogen and helium gas floated through space, and it took another two hundred million years for those gas clouds to produce the first stars. This was when the lights of the universe were turned on, so to speak. One billion years after the big bang, the first galaxy formed, and over the next eight billion years, countless more took shape. Then, about five billion years ago, in a quiet corner of an unassuming spiral galaxy, gravity began to draw in dust and gas. Gradually, the gas clumped together and created a star—our sun. Nine billion years after the Big Bang, our solar system sprang to life.

Everything there is exists because of the Big Bang. But wait a minute; if the Big Bang only produced hydrogen, helium, and lithium, where did all the other elements come from? Well, the answer lies in the stars.

Our sun has been lighting our solar system for the last 4.6 billion years and in terms of size, our sun is a dwarf. There are real monster-sized stars out there, millions of times bigger than our sun. Stars all start out the same way, in clouds of dust and gas called nebulae. These nebulae are also known as star nurseries where millions of stars are born. Gravity pulls in enormous amounts of hydrogen gas over hundreds of thousands of years until the heat and pressure in the core of this massive ball of swirling gas reaches a critical point. This critical point is when the heat in the core reaches fifteen million degrees. Only at this temperature can atoms of gas fuse together, and in the process, release massive amounts of energy in the form of heat and radiation.

So stars are nuclear fusion engines. When hydrogen atoms fuse, a new element is created—helium—along with a small amount of pure energy. Because helium weighs slightly less than hydrogen, there is a loss in mass in the fusion process, and this loss in mass is turned into energy. Gravity compresses the outer layers of the star while the energy of fusion wants to blow the star apart. These forces are at odds during the duration of a star's life.

Our sun burns or fuses six hundred million tons of the hydrogen gas at its core every second. At this rate the sun will run out of fuel in about seven billion years. As the hydrogen fuel is used up, it slows down the fusion process at its core. With less outward force, gravity will crush the star in on itself. But this crushing force will heat up the remaining gasses at the core even more, and the sun will expand to become a red giant and eventually engulf the Earth.

But the giant red star will destroy itself. With no hydrogen left to fuel it, the sun will begin to fuse helium into carbon. Violent surges of energy will blast from the core to the surface and blow away the star's outer layers. Slowly it will disintegrate. All that remains will be an intensely hot and dense core; the sun will be a white dwarf, and the fusion process will have stopped. Our sun will then be the size of the Earth. Some astronomers believe that at the heart of a white dwarf is a giant crystal of pure carbon—a diamond thousands of miles across. (Can anyone sing "Lucy in the Sky with Diamonds"?)

The death of massive stars creates the building blocks of the universe as they create pressures and temperatures at their cores greater than anywhere else in the universe. The pressures at the core of massive stars are so powerful they can fuse bigger and bigger atoms. This produces the element iron, and iron absorbs energy. So the moment a massive star creates iron, it has only seconds to live. The star is trying to fuse iron, but it can't, and fusion stops abruptly. Gravity wins. The iron core collapses, and the outer layers of the star slams into it. A massive explosion is generated—a supernova explosion.

In just a second, supernova explosions create more energy than our sun ever will. Material from the core of the star travels outward. In the extreme heat and turmoil of the explosion, heavier elements are created—among them gold, silver, and platinum—and because there is so little time for the elements to form, they are the rarest and most valuable in the universe. The dying star blasts the new elements far out into space—like hydrogen, carbon, oxygen, silicon, and iron—which are needed to build new stars, solar systems, and planets.

Everything we see around us was once stardust. Even the atoms in our bodies were created inside the core of a dying star.

After many weeks of reading, I was satisfied with my concise rundown of the coming into being of the universe. I found the processes and forces at work in the universe elegant and mesmerizing, but what struck me most was the thought that I am the result of the universe trying to understand what exactly the universe is. I could describe cosmic, stellar, chemical, and planetary evolution as a product of all those processes.

After weeks of not being present in class, I was told by one of my classmates that my psychology professor (a civilian) wanted to see me in her office immediately, as she had picked up on the fact that I was absent, and she wanted an explanation. She didn't raise her voice once, but spoke to me like a disappointed mother would speak to a son who did something very stupid. Apparently my military file indicated that my father had committed suicide, and after a good ten minutes of making me feel that I was the worst human being imaginable, she wanted to know how I was dealing with his death. I hated her then. In an instant she made me return to a reality I didn't want to acknowledge. I assured her that I would never miss one of her classes again, turned around, and walked out of her office.

I knew something had to be done. I could not let my anger, frustration, broken heart, and bad temper ruin my studies and my career. I don't quite know why I decided to try my hand at horseback riding, but I began to visit the military academy equestrian club regularly after my uncomfortable encounter with my psychology professor. And that's when I met Panther.

Panther was a giant among horses and had a temperament to go with it. He was also big, black, and frightening. And instead of having a kind streak, Panther had a meanness to him that should not be contained in an animal. I had heard rumors around the stables that Panther had been used in Operation Boleas, a military operation launched in September 1998 by the Southern African Development Community to quell a suspected coup d'état in the landlocked Kingdom of Lesotho. Troops from Botswana were supposed to join South African defense forces, but the Botswana contingent lost its way, and only South African troops crossed the border.

Because of the mountainous terrain, mounted soldiers formed part of the contingent, and the rumor was that Panther's rider was killed in an ambush. I had no idea how true this rumor was, but I know enough about rumors to know that they are often exaggerated and even more regularly completely false. Whatever the reason for Panther's temperament, it made life for me very difficult, as I never stayed on his back for very long. But I liked the fact that Panther taught me lesson after lesson.

Some days I would just talk to him and explain that even the atoms in his hooves were created in the core of star and that one day when he died his atoms would return to the Earth and become part of something else. But my final success came in the form of carrots and apples. I believe he began to associate me with carrots and apples, and slowly I began to eat less dust. After one particular day of riding and falling, of falling and crawling, of screaming and shouting, of carrots and apples, Panther and I seemed to have found each other. We even went for a ride on the beach.

I will never know why Panther was so violent at first, but after several weekends the glint of anger behind his eyes grew faint. Yet my reflection in his eyes remained dark and angry. Panther was a saint; I was a beast.

The senior graduation parade took place a week after the last exam was written, and when it was over I went to a special place on the beach to be alone for a while. There was no one in sight except a fisherman standing on the rocks with his fishing rod in his hands. No civilians are allowed on the base without proper authorization, and I remember thinking that I should report him to base security as soon as I left the beach. I stood there and looked across the ocean at nothing in particular. Navy had graduated and left the academy just after the parade had finished. We never said good-bye. I looked at the seagulls gliding on the breeze, and for one moment I thought that they were accusing me: "You killed your father! You killed your father!" There was no way of knowing then that only a little more than two years later the seagulls in the Highlands of Scotland would come to mean something very different.

Out of the corner of my eye, I saw the fisherman walking up to me. I was uneasy at first, but decided not to move. He stood next to me and seemed to be trying to see what I was looking at across the ocean. He looked more than a hundred years old, and he had very few teeth left in his mouth. He stank of dried sweat, fish, and cheap wine. Without warning he spoke. "Sorry, master, but the horizon ain't gonna tell you nothing. It doesn't have the answers you are looking for."

I looked at him with disgust. "I'm not your master."

"Aagh, it's just the way us fishermen speak on the west coast. Don't get your panties in a twist about it."

"So, what answers am I looking for then?" I asked.

"A man with that look on his face has either lost his God or his woman. Love is a funny thing, master. If you look for it, you won't find it. Love finds you. All you can do in the meantime is drink like a fish and hope you win the lotto. There are plenty of fish in the sea, master, but who wants a fish when he can have a mermaid? God made everything two by two, master. Your mermaid is still in the water."

"And if I lost my God?"

"Woo, that is something entirely different master. Maybe you should become a fisherman like me. Jesus seemed to like fishermen. Maybe then he will come looking for you. By the way, master, do you have a smoke for me? I forgot mine at home."

It felt as if he knew me, as if he had known me all my life. Him! A semi-sober fisherman! Something began to move inside me then. I didn't understand that movement at first, but it felt familiar in some way. I breathed in deeply and then I recognized the movement: the tides inside me that had shuddered to a standstill more than six months previously had returned. I felt their slow and faint rhythm, and my broken heart from a romantic failure began to mend. My mermaid was still in the water.

I gave the fisherman all the cigarettes I had left and looked at him for a while as he sauntered back to his fishing rod, astonished at his ability to look past all my defenses and pretenses and see my heart. I didn't report him to base security.

# 7

# Lady Killer

*There is a theory which states that if ever anyone discovers exactly what the Universe is for and why it is here, it will instantly disappear and be replaced by something even more bizarre and inexplicable.*
*There is another theory which states that this has already happened.*

—DOUGLAS ADAMS

*(The Restaurant at the End of the Universe)*

My senior year at the military academy started like the two previous ones—with a morning parade. Lecturers and students greeted each other in the halls in the faculty building, and at night friends sat around talking about what they did during the holiday. Life at the academy was predictable—morning parades, classes, fitness tests, shooting exercises, exams—and the predictability made everybody feel at ease. First-year students were nervous (as they should be); second-year students were arrogant; and third-years ruled the tiny universe that we called home. Life at the academy was paradise to a man who needed solitude.

I attended services at the base chapel on Sundays, but only because I'd bought a drum set at the beginning of that year and inadvertently became the drummer in the church band. My father had shown me a picture once of him sitting behind a drum set with the name of their band in big letters on the front skin of the kick drum: The Star Knights. I don't know if skill can be transferred from father to son, but playing the drums came very easily. I just sat behind the set and started to play, and it transported me to a place and time where my father was still with me in some way. I loved that drum set. And going to services on Sundays was a purely social event for me.

Even though I had begun to attend classes since that day with my psychology professor, I still did my own thing at night. Of course, some nights would drag on far too long, which meant that I missed a few classes in the morning, but I didn't miss my psychology professor's class. I thought it best to keep my word.

I was still satisfied with my concise rundown of the creation of the universe, and the next topic on my agenda was the origin of life and evolution. But after some thought one night, I realized that I could explain only the *growth* of the universe after creation but not *why* the universe came into being. This realization made me acknowledge the fact that the first issue or question I had to answer was "Does God exist?" I had many more questions, like "What is the meaning of life?" "What is the origin of life?" "Why am I here?" "Do I have a purpose?" and "Do I have any intrinsic value?" Although these questions are important in their own right, I would first have to come to some sort of reasonable conclusion to the question "Does God exist?"

If, for instance, I was already dedicated to the idea that nothing can exist outside the universe and that there is no ultimate supernatural force responsible for its creation, my response to the question "Does God exist?" would have to be no. The atheistic viewpoint is that there is no God and that the universe just exists. The universe wasn't created by a supernatural force with intent or design, and life is just the result of a series of random, happy chemical accidents; given the right circumstances, life just happens.

If that were the case, there would be no sense in answering any of the other questions. There would be no ultimate meaning of life; life is just life. There would be no ultimate purpose to life; it is just a natural consequence of the chemical evolution of a planet. Everything is just the result of random cosmic events with no true design or purpose; we are here by tremendous and fantastic accident. But the statements "God exists" and "God doesn't exist" are both statements of faith, because the existence of God cannot be proven or disproven from an evidentiary standpoint within our natural realm. These are the issues that have been on the mind of humankind for millennia, but I was willing to approach them with an open mind.

In 1859, English naturalist Charles Darwin published *On the Origin of Species,* in which he put forward the theory that life is descended over time from common ancestry through a process he called natural selection: the preservation of beneficial random genetic mutations within an organism's genetic code because they aid in the organism's survival. It is important, however, to keep in mind that Darwin's theory only attempts to explain why there is such diversity among species; it doesn't explain or solve where life came from in the first place.

The atheist believes that just because something is unexplained, it doesn't imply a creator or designer; rather, say it isn't explained yet, and science will find the answer eventually. The atheist feels that the absence of evidence for the existence of God is evidence for His absence. But the believer feels that the absence of evidence for the existence of God is *not* evidence for His absence; evidence for God's existence can be found in the rational operation of the universe according to certain laws and constants.

These thoughts plagued me to the point of exploding into a puff of smoke. Although I was present in class, I may as well have been thousands of miles away, as I was only present in body; my mind was somewhere else. I tried to keep the entirety of events in mind—that is, after the Big Bang, multiple constants and forces were just right for the universe to take shape and produce what we experience today; gravity had just the right value; there was more matter than antimatter; and there was a nonuniform distribution of mass for gravity to act on and pull in clouds of gas so that stars could form and in turn produce other elements. These elements would later become the chemical ingredients for the formation of amino acids and complex proteins necessary for the generation of organisms on a planet that happens to be far enough away from its star so that water can exist in a liquid state.

This planet also has a core of spinning liquid iron that produces a magnetic field around it that conveniently protects the evolving living organisms on the planet from harmful electromagnetic radiation emitted from its star. This planet also just so happens to be part of a solar system with a large gas planet, called Jupiter, that acts as a cosmic vacuum cleaner by sucking up objects like comets and asteroids that might be heading on a collision course with it. And after billions of years of evolution by means of natural selection, a species emerges that has a personality, has emotions, can reason with its mind, create art, love, ponder the meaning of existence, and describe the universe it lives in elegantly by means of mathematics, because the universe also just so happens to be rational, operating according to certain laws.

I had reasonable doubt that all this happened naturally without design, intent, and direction. Thinking that it just happened by accident is analogous to thinking that if you take all the different parts of an Airbus A-380—the millions of rivets, the engine parts, the electronic and avionic instruments, all the wiring—and put them in the world's biggest tumble dryer and set it to a cycle of 13.7 billion years, you would find an assembled and fully functional jet plane when you eventually open the door. The odds of this happening all by itself are simply impossible to comprehend or calculate.

Of course, the atheist would reason that the odds of this happening spontaneously is very good, because it happened at least once already—in fact, we are experiencing it right now. Perhaps I am just not smart enough and perhaps I don't possess enough power of reason, but I suspect that an accidental Airbus A-380 isn't nearly as complex and beautiful as our universe.

As far as our sense of morality goes, there are only two options to choose from: On one hand, our moral sense of right and wrong is just another product of evolution; it is a remnant of the herd instinct, and later, when humans began to live in small groups, of societal preferences that you not steal, kill, or lie and that you contribute to the group. Or, on the other hand, we can believe that our sense of morality is derived from God, who is a moral law giver. He is ultimate morality and ultimate justice.

If I believe that objective morality is just another product of evolution, where nature weeds out the weak and prefers that the strong survive, I cannot reason that what Hitler did was ultimately wrong. He was merely the product of a natural process, and in terms of survival-of-the-fittest, Hitler merely asserted his strength and eradicated those he perceived as weak and inferior. We would have *preferred* that it never happen, but it is just the nature of existence. If there is no ultimate moral lawgiver, there would be no ultimate justice, compensation, or consolation. There would be no ultimate justice for the abused, the forgotten, the abandoned, the downtrodden, the meek, and the weak.

For example, there would be no ultimate justice for an eight-month-old baby who was gang raped by four men in South Africa because they were convinced that having sex with a minor and a virgin was a cure for HIV/AIDS. The public outcry in South Africa, and indeed around the world, was astounding. The authorities had to step in and prevent the community from tearing those men apart like a pack of wild dogs. But many consoled themselves with the thought that she didn't experience pain for very long, before she lost consciousness.

If I don't believe in an ultimate moral lawgiver, I will have to somehow find it in myself to come to terms with the statement "Life sucks and then you die." That baby will one day have to come to terms with the same thing. What will we say to that little girl when she is old enough to understand? Will we sit her down and tell her that there is no God and that there is no mind or intelligence behind the universe? Will we tell her that everything is just the result of a mindless, unintelligent accident? We can provide her with reconstructive surgery, but we will have to explain that she will never be able to have children and that as an adult she will never be able to enjoy sex because she was torn apart too severely. We will have to tell her that there are bad people in this world and that sometimes people are just unlucky. We will have to explain that she can find only short-term, subjective meaning and purpose in her life because she wasn't created for a divine purpose. We will have to explain that because the prisons are overcrowded, the men who raped her before she could even talk will probably be released in fifteen years.

We will also explain that we live in a world where some corporate executives are awarded bonuses upwards of ten million dollars, but that she will probably never earn more than a thousand dollars a year because she was born to a poor family—but that it is really okay, because we call it capitalism and we think *capitalism* is a good word. We will tell her that she is now infected with an incurable disease and that her suffering will finally be over when she dies, because after death there is nothing.

Will you be the one to tell her this because there is no evidence for the existence for God? Or will you be the one to tell her that there is always hope in God, that you don't have any evidence for his existence, but that there are hints that He exists all around us—from mitosis to nuclear fusion in the core of a star to the preservation of beneficial genetic mutations? You will tell her that someday she will be taken up and enveloped in an ultimate and infinite personal love—the kind of love that, if it flutters just a little, causes universes to spring into existence with an energy that can never be quantified. You will explain to her that love was never created; it has always existed and it can never be destroyed. You will tell her that love is just another word for God.

I struggled for weeks with creationism and evolutionism, in the sense that I had to choose one of them. Many, if not all religions, reject evolutionism because it negates God as a creator, but I found the mechanism of evolution so very intriguing, almost beautiful; it is a natural force at work on the genetic level that produces complexity in organisms in order to ensure the survival of the species.

And then, one day, while I was talking to Panther and feeding him apples, a thought slowly invaded my mind: if I believe that God created the universe and that He is the artificer of the natural laws, wouldn't it stand to reason that He is also the artificer of natural selection? Could it be conceivable that in the moment of creation, natural selection was a purposeful and designed intent that would eventually give rise to the human species—one that would eventually lead to me feeding an apple to a horse? *Congratulations, Neil,* I thought, *You have just removed the sting of evolution, and people will throw stones at you for as long as you live—religious and atheist alike—because you just created a new philosophical ism: creatovolutionism.* I had had enough then and decided to leave creation vs. evolution alone for good, because I believed in both. I am now a deist. I am not a Christian, Jew, or Muslim. I am just a man who believes that God exists. I believed in a creator.

I was totally exhausted by thoughts of God and existence and morality. I was tired of reading articles and spending countless nights pondering the existence of God and the creation of the universe. The philosophical and metaphysical questions had drained my strength.

It was around this time that poetry began to approach me again, but this time it arrived as a weapon. I used poetry to get girls, and I am ashamed to say that it worked more often than not. For most of my senior year, I pursued girls like a starving bushman pursues an antelope. But the true colors of the darkness inside me proved to be a terrible thing. For fear of suffering from a broken heart again, I was the one who broke hearts. Every time, I simply walked away without giving any reason or explanation. Needless to say, after a while I had acquired somewhat of a reputation as a "lady killer," as they put it. I was someone bound to take a woman in and spit her out—as if she were nothing but a toy to play with until it became too serious or too close for comfort. Soon enough I decided to concentrate on my studies and obtain good grades instead.

At the end of 2000 I obtained a B-Mil degree in human sciences. Looking back on my three years of study at the military academy and constant grooming for a future career with endless leadership courses, I think I know enough about leadership now to know that in extreme circumstances, people will follow just because someone else says, "Follow me." But I also know that true leadership is about winning people's hearts. I know that respect is earned and that honor is more than just a word; it is a lifestyle. I know that insignia says nothing about an individual's values and that bravery is sometimes motivated by fear. When bullets fly and bombs explode, soldiers don't fight for a creed or politics; in the heat of battle, they fight to stay alive.

I wasn't ready to leave the academy just yet, so I applied to stay on for another year to complete a post-graduate degree in computer information systems. I needed more solitude.

# 8

# War Orphan

*I like your Christ. I do not like your Christians.*
*Your Christians are so unlike your Christ*

—MAHATMA GANDHI

If being a senior at the military academy felt like ruling a tiny universe, then being a post-graduate student felt a lot like being a demigod. No more early-morning parades; those were for the rabble. No more shooting exercises; those were for the commoners. No more standing in line during breakfast, lunch, and supper; that was for the back-of-liners.

I realized that I would never be able to know why God created the universe. We can come to some sort of conclusion as to the existence of God, but the question of why he created the universe will have to be answered by knowing the mind of God, and that is impossible. I did, however, imagine that I could travel back in time with a time machine to meet Shakespeare and that when I met him, I would ask him why he wrote that very first poem when he was still unknown. There was no possibility for him to make money from it, and though the value of the poem would be contained only within the words, it would only have subjective meaning. Perhaps Shakespeare was very young at the time, just like I was only sixteen years old when I wrote my first faint lines. I suspect that Shakespeare's answer would be a lot like mine: "I wrote because I just couldn't help myself. I had to do it." Although Shakespeare's works are impressive, to say the least, his creativity was still limited. Now imagine infinite creativity. Perhaps the answer to why God created the universe is similar. But I am simply guessing and letting my mind wonder.

Most of the last conversations Zulu and I had were about him wanting to volunteer to go to Burundi. South Africa, along with other SADC (Southern African Development Community) countries, was participating in a peacekeeping mission in that country, but I had seen a military video about the war in Rwanda, so I knew that war in Africa wasn't a pretty thing. Seeing someone get shot in a movie is one thing, but seeing someone get shot for real on camera is something entirely different—no special effects, just pain, blood, and death. In general, bullets were too expensive, so to cut costs, people were simply burned, hacked, and chopped to death. After all, a machete needs no maintenance.

Many South African soldiers had various reasons for wanting to go to Burundi: some wanted the "danger pay" and extra allowances and some wanted the experience. But when I asked Zulu why he wanted to go, he simply replied, "Jesus loves that country too. And besides, I'm a pretty big guy; maybe I can help tame the mad elephant of war."

In "Military Strategy" class during my second year, most of our focus was about the changing role of the South African National Defence Force. In the absence of an enemy, war was the enemy itself. I remember one student asking our professor why South African soldiers should risk life and limb to protect people they did not love and fighting those they did not hate. His reply made an impact on me: "We have the ability to respond; therefore we have a responsibility."

I didn't want Zulu to get hurt, but I knew that once he set his mind on something there would be no changing it. Why was it so easy for him to say, "Jesus loves this country"? Why was it so easy for him to look to the north and say, "Jesus loves that country too"?

I was more than happy with just remaining a deist, and this made me realize that I had a fundamental problem with religion as a whole: over the centuries, we have somehow managed to put God in a box and wrap it in multiple layers of tradition, dogma, and religism—so much so, that we have effectively *organized* God out of organized religion. I also could not stand religion because of what it makes us do to each other. Religion is what makes a man strap a bomb to his chest so that he can blow himself and all those around him up in the name of the God of his religion. It's what makes a man blow up an abortion clinic and everybody inside it, because that is what the God of his religion would want.

So I felt repulsed by religion. I was revolted by the people who claimed God as a participant and an accomplice in violent acts, saying that God condones these acts as long as we do it for the right reason (and in His name). I honestly felt that religion made reasonable people ignorant, blind, and stupid. It was simply morality touched by emotion, and over the centuries religion has devolved into modern-day tribalism, an us-against-them attitude: if I am a follower of one religion, then all others are wrong and to hell with them, literally. If I had been born in Saudi Arabia to Muslim parents—a country where Bibles are outlawed—I would be a Muslim right now. If I had been born in Japan, I would be either Shinto or Buddhist. Or in India, I would be Hindu. So in many ways, religion, much like culture, comes down to geographical location on the planet, and this is something we have no control over; we are just born. I also could have been born to nonreligious parents.

But I wasn't born to any of these. I was born to Christian parents in South Africa, and that makes me unique (as unique as all others born to Christian parents in South Africa). The biggest problem I had with Christianity was many of its Christians, and the same can be said for Islam.

One day, in Cape Town, I walked into a bookstore and bought an English translation of the Quran (actually one of those where the pages are split down the middle with Arabic on the one side and English on the other). I took it home with me and started to read it just like I would read the Bible. The drummer in the church band could not be caught with a Quran in his room, so I carefully hid it behind my textbooks on the bookshelf.

I tried my best to memorize the ninety-nine beautiful names of God—the Exceedingly Merciful, the Provider, the King, the Creator, and so on—and for a short while, as I sat in class, I recited those names to the best of my ability. (I never could quite remember more than a few). But it struck me early on that it was very similar to the Bible, and reading the Quran quickly proved to be a futile exercise; it didn't last more than a few weeks.

I was reminded of a staff sergeant I worked with at Air Force Headquarters while I was still a noncommissioned officer. He was a Muslim (the first one I had known), and I could not help but admire his commitment to quit smoking for the duration of Ramadan. When Ramadan was over, he quickly resumed smoking. But the point I'm trying to make is that he believed what he believed with conviction. He was a good soldier, a good husband, and a good father. (I also recall that he was one of the funniest people I have ever shared an office with.)

The problem that I had with Christianity—and Islam, for that matter—was the people who would judge and condemn without hesitation: "All nonbelievers should burn" or "God hates infidels." The Christians who show up at soldiers' funerals holding up placards that read "God hates fags!" The Muslim protester who holds up a poster that reads "Death to the west! Death to the infidel!" The man who sits in church every Sunday while quietly addicted to child-pornography. The man who beats his wife, and when she wants to leave him, cooks up a story about adultery and delivers her to the utter torment of sentencing under Sharia law (which, in some countries, is death through beheading). I couldn't stand religion. I hated it! Religion was not love!

Christians believe in the divinity of Christ, but so many Christians are not Christians at all but mere fans. The church they go to is like a fan club to them. I know what I'm talking about, because I was the drummer in my fan club.

Around this time, a few months before the end of the year, I had to research and write a thesis about knowledge and information management in the South African Department of Defence and how such a system should be implemented. This was a requirement for my post-graduate degree, and it required a lot of research on the Internet. During one of those many lengthy Internet searches, I came upon a book titled *On the Incarnation of the Word*, written by St. Athanasius. I promptly downloaded it so that I could take it to my room and read it at my leisure.

Since thinking about religion, many questions had come to mind that bothered me as background noise in the jumble of my thoughts, and I never quite knew how I was ever going to find answers to those questions: Can I believe the Gospels? Did Jesus even exist? What if everything is just a big, fat lie?

It took many weeks for me to read *On the Incarnation of the Word*, perhaps even more than a month, and when I was done with it, I was suspicious. Perhaps I could believe the Gospels. Perhaps everything was not a big, fat lie. So I made a simple, fleeting choice: if anyone ever asked me again, I would say that I was a Christian. Perhaps that was as close as I was ever going to get. Athanasius's book was simply written in the form of a letter (like so many books were back then)—a letter from one man to another discussing a subject: the divinity of Christ. I liked that book (and I still do). In today's world, that book could have been a recording of a three-hour telephone conversation between two people: the one wiser with experience and the other a willing listener.

But the choice I made lacked something. It lacked knowledge and personal experience of God, and I knew I was going to have to fake it as a Christian. I didn't make that choice with conviction. To be honest, I made it because I was tired. Nothing that I read moved me. Nothing a pastor or priest or minister ever said moved me. I simply had to be moved because nothing else was going to get me there. And failing that, I was going to have to fake it. And knowing myself, I was quickly going to get tired of faking it and be right back where I started.

Seeing that Athanasius's book reminded me of a modern-day recorded telephone conversation, I thought to call Zulu again to see what he was up to. I even thought that this time I was going to bring God into the conversation to see what his thoughts were on some of the questions I had.

His cell phone went straight to voicemail on the first day, but it wasn't uncommon for soldiers to be out of reach when they were away on training, so I didn't think much of it. I gave it a few days and tried to call him again that weekend—voicemail again. When he was unavailable the next weekend, I decided I would call his squadron personnel officer on Monday to find out when Zulu would be back from training.

But he wasn't away on training.

The personnel officer informed that Zulu was dead—a victim of a senseless crime. He had taken some leave and was on his way to visit his mother in the Kwa-Zulu Natal Highlands when he was attacked by three men and thrown from a moving train. He didn't die a hero trying to tame the mad elephant of war in a foreign country that God also apparently loved. Instead he died right there beside the tracks.

The friend I made that night under a tree so many years ago was gone. My heart was totally and utterly destroyed. Zulu had been buried the week before near his mother's village. His attackers got away with his shoes and his wallet.

I was in a daze. It felt unreal. I researched and wrote my thesis. I studied for exams. I slept. I ate. I woke. I called his cell phone many times simply to hear his recorded voice until it, too, was dead and gone.

A couple of months before graduation, I wanted to do something special in his memory and decided on monthly financial pledges for the care of war-orphans in Burundi. It was the closest I could get him to that country. It was the closest I could get him to being a hero. Later I began to send e-mails to the organization that cared for the orphans as well. They were just short, nonsensical e-mails about my life at the military academy and how I don't seem to be able to stay on a horse. I think a part of me was sending those e-mails to Zulu.

And then I graduated.

# 9

# SINGLE MALT COUNTRY

*It is a curious thing, the death of a loved one. We all know that our time in this world is limited, and that eventually all of us will end up underneath some sheet, never to wake up. And yet it is always a surprise when it happens to someone we know. It is like walking up the stairs to your bedroom in the dark, and thinking there is one more stair than there is. Your foot falls down, through the air, and there is a sickly moment of dark surprise as you try and readjust the way you thought of things.*

—LEMONY SNICKET

(*Horseradish: Bitter Truths You Can't Avoid*)

After graduation I was transferred to a post in Pretoria, where I worked in an underground fortified bunker known to all who worked there simply as Blenny. The thick concrete, big blast doors, and recirculated air perfectly resembled what my heart must have looked like. I quickly missed the fresh air of Saldanha, the seagulls, the beach, and my tiny room on the third floor. I missed the equestrian club, impromptu barbecues with friends, and the ability to be completely alone by simply going for a walk. My soul was slowly and truly dying.

I resigned my commission in the Air Force on a Wednesday morning, six months after my arrival at my new post. I had grown increasingly restless since Zulu's death and found it very hard to pretend that I didn't miss him. I found it hard to accept that I would never get a call from him again, asking me how I was doing and what I was up to. Perhaps I felt guilty knowing that I was never really a good friend to him. I had called on important dates like birthdays and holidays, but in terms of keeping our friendship alive, he was the one who made the effort. I was distraught over his loss, and it left me feeling adrift. I knew that I would never meet someone like him again, and it was something I should have told him while he was still alive.

Whether it was anger or sadness or guilt that made me resign isn't really important. I resigned because I simply had to get away from Africa, if only for a while. I sold everything I owned (except my motorcycle) and went to England three months later with a backpack and a hole in my heart.

Arriving at Heathrow International Airport that day in London brought what felt like relief. For the first time, I knew what it felt like to be truly anonymous. I looked English, and with a little bit of effort I even sounded English. No one walking past me in the arrivals terminal paid me any attention. No one asked me what my name was or what I did for a living. No one asked me how I was doing or what I was thinking. No one knew that I was trying to keep the memory of a friend alive by sending money and an e-mail every month so that orphans can live. No one suspected that I didn't return my father's phone call the night before he ended his life.

I will never forget those first few minutes in the arrivals terminal. I was just another man waiting for his luggage. I could have been anyone. I could have been the man on his way to an important business meeting (although I wasn't dressed for the part). I could have been the man who came to visit his family or his girlfriend or his wife. I could have been anyone that day, and the thought was soothing. But although I was six thousand miles away from home, my heart was unaware that I was no longer on the African continent, and it would soon remind me of this fact.

I had arranged to stay with a friend who worked in a pub in Chigwell. After spending about half an hour trying to figure out what train would take me where, I finally boarded one headed for the eastern outskirts of London.

I had only enough money to last me about three days, so I had to find a job in a hurry, but luckily someone at the pub gave me the number of an agent in London who found work for people on farms. After making a call, I obtained the number of a farmer in Kent who needed someone for the harvest season. The farmer and I had a quick telephonic interview, and when he asked me if I had any experience on tractors, I only had to look in the direction of my wallet and what little money I had left to find an answer. "Yes, lots," I lied.

Driving a tractor is easy, not much unlike driving a car. It has a clutch, a brake pedal—and to my complete horror, twelve gears. When the farmer went to bed on my very first night on the farm, I snuck out of my mobile cabin with a flashlight, got into the tractor, and "reverse engineered" whatever I needed to know. The pictograms for the semiautomatic gearbox helped a lot: "Rabbit for fast and tortoise for slow," I told myself.

I loved the hard work, and the farmer made sure that he worked me like a slave, but I welcomed it. Keeping busy kept me from going insane. I worked thirteen to sixteen hours a day, seven days a week, and I loved it. Most of my days on that farm consisted of carting grain from the field back to the grain store. Some days I worked in the grain store shoveling grain like there was no tomorrow. For some reason I liked the idea of having blisters on my hands when I went to bed at night, perhaps because having pain on the outside of my body made me forget about the pain on the inside.

After work, I would spend about an hour in the shower struggling to get the grain dust out of my hair or washing the tractor's hydraulic fluid from my body. Then I cooked a quick dinner and fell asleep, exhausted. In the mornings, I would meet the farmer in the yard at five o'clock, and we would discuss what needed to be done that day. If it included carting grain with the tractor and trailer, I would be especially excited, because it meant I got to drive through small villages I had never seen or heard of before, like Tenterden, Bethersden, Woodchurch—little, rustic, country villages with a church, a cemetery, and three pubs.

The farmer only needed someone for seven weeks, and after my last day of work, he wrote me a check and took me to the train station in Ashford. I will never forget that first paycheck; in just seven weeks I had managed to save a small fortune. When I arrived in London, I asked around for a youth hostel and eventually found a room in one in Hyde Park.

I stayed in the youth hostel for one week of rest before deciding to find another job. I called the same agent in London, and he provided me with the details of a greenhouse owner who needed a worker. I called the owner, made arrangements, and the following morning I was on a train headed for Surrey.

Again I stayed in a mobile cabin on the premises, but at least this time I had a black-and-white television to keep me company at night. My duties at the greenhouse consisted of delivering flowers, planting seedlings, trimming hedges, and pulling up weeds; it was not rocket science, but it kept me busy. I had a day off on Wednesdays, and on those days I would walk to the library in the village to use the Internet so I could send money and an e-mail to the organization that cared for war orphans in Burundi.

But on one of these days I found that I was the recipient of an e-mail:

> Dear Mr. Davies,
>
> I have never been to South Africa, but have heard it said that it is a very beautiful country. I trust that you are well and that you are successful in your endeavors.
>
> I have received all your e-mails and enjoyed reading them very much. Later, I began to read them to one particular six-year-old girl who had a very special place in my heart. She was one of the first who came to stay with us.
>
> It wasn't easy to explain to such a young soul where South Africa is, but she seemed to be content with the explanation that it is a place very far to the south. Equally, it wasn't easy to explain to her who you are, but again, she seemed to be content with the explanation that you are a good man who cares about her. She especially enjoyed the letters in which you described your adventures with horses. She has never seen a horse and found it very peculiar that a man could sit on an animal, much less ride one.

> It is with the deepest sorrow that I inform you that she has died as a result of AIDS a few days ago. We teach all the orphans in our care about Jesus and baptize as many of them as we can. We teach them how to pray and although some of them are very young and do not understand a word, I believe that the soul has an unspoken language. I tried to explain what death was and what would happen to her after she had gone as best I could, and she very much liked the thought of heaven.
>
> I was with her to the end and it is here that I want to relate her finest hour with wondrous joy. She told me that she wasn't afraid and that she was looking forward to staying with you and playing with horses. You see Mr. Davies, in her innocence she thought that the letters I read to her once a month were in fact written by Jesus. May God forgive me, but I didn't want to confuse or disappoint her in her final moments and told her that you will receive her with open arms.
>
> Thank you for revealing heaven to a little girl.
>
> Your servant in God,
>
> M.

I sat in front of that computer for a very long time. The people around me were reading books or newspapers as if a little life hadn't expired a few days ago. I just sat there and stared at the computer screen. I didn't want to read the e-mail again, but I couldn't help it and read it over and over.

Sending e-mails and money once a month had been the one thing I held on to that made me feel better about a great many things, but now even that was taken away. I didn't feel anger or frustration or pain in that moment; I felt nothing, and feeling nothing is much worse than feeling emotional or physical pain. I would have given anything in that moment to feel sadness or pain. Eventually I printed a copy of the letter, logged off, and walked out of the library. I didn't send any more money or e-mails after that day.

When I got back to the greenhouse, I packed my things and walked to the train station. I didn't tell the owner that I was leaving or even collected my last paycheck; I just left. I obtained a room in the same youth hostel in London for just one night, and the next morning took a taxi to the Victoria bus station. When I walked into the terminal, I went up to the ticket office, pointed to a bus that was preparing to leave, and asked, "Excuse me, sir, can you tell me where that bus is going?"

The ticket clerk looked at me with a frown and said, "Sure, it's going to Inverness."

"And where is that exactly?"

"It's in the Highlands of Scotland, lad. If you want a ticket, you better hurry, because the bus will be leaving soon."

I paid forty pounds for a one-way ticket, stored my backpack in the trailer, and settled in for a twelve-hour drive to the Highlands of Scotland—and hopefully oblivion. I fell asleep for a long time and woke up just in time to read a road sign. It said, "Now entering single malt country."

*Great,* I thought. *Where I'm going there's lots of whiskey.* And then I closed my eyes again.

# 10

## Seagulls and God-Talk

*In every young man's life there is a "Selma" who appears to him suddenly while in the spring of life and transforms his solitude into happy moments and fills the silence of his nights with music.*

—KHALIL GIBRAN

*(The Broken Wings)*

Arriving in Inverness felt a lot like that day at Heathrow Airport. Again I felt anonymous. I asked for directions at the information kiosk inside the bus station and eventually found a room in a youth hostel on the main street. Most youth hostels have bulletin boards that advertise work, and as I walked to my room on the second floor, I took down the number of a local salmon processing plant that was looking for people—people just like me (to date, it is the only job I have had that actually required me to come to work with my own knife).

In my room, I sat on the bed for a while and allowed myself to take in the situation. I was as far north as I have ever been; any farther and I would end up in the Arctic. I tried to imagine myself in the Arctic, working at some research facility drilling ice core samples. I could do that too (or maybe not).

I removed my sleeping bag from my backpack and rolled it out on the bed. When I lifted the pillow, I found a book—a well-worn Quran. Someone must have left it there, another backpacker. I was reminded of the ninety-nine beautiful names of God—the Exceedingly Merciful, the King, the Creator—but those names meant nothing to me, and I tossed it in the trashcan with a casual fling. *God is not going to follow me to Scotland,* I thought. I would have done the same if I had found a Bible under the pillow.

There weren't many people staying in the hostel. I suppose being that far north and being so far away from all the big cities didn't attract many people. There were a few guys and girls from Australia (Aussies seem to be everywhere), three girls from Canada, a couple from Brazil, four guys from Germany, two French girls, and another girl who seemed to be English, although she looked Brazilian as well. I would later learn that she was half Lebanese. For this reason and for the purposes of this book, her name shall be Lebanon.

The job at the salmon processing plant suited me just fine. I worked from five in the evening until three in the mornings, packing fish. When I got back to the hostel, I would go to the kitchen and make myself a cup of coffee, and then I would go to the lounge and sit in front of the fireplace with a book. I had read Charles Dickens's *David Copperfield* many times, and when I found it in the bookshelf in the lounge, I took it as a sign that I have come to the right place. At six in the mornings, when the other people in the hostel started to rise, I would take a shower and go to bed.

I loved it! I loved the peace and quiet. Nobody bothered me. For just a few hours, the fireplace in the lounge belonged to me. For just a few hours, the Highlands of Scotland belonged to me. Every day I had a few hours just to myself.

Lebanon came into my life like a whirlwind or like lightning. I came back to the hostel one morning after a particularly hard shift and was looking forward to sitting in front of the fireplace (it was very cold in Scotland that time of year). I made a cup of coffee, went to the lounge, and to my dismay found someone sitting in my chair. From the back of her head and her long, dark hair hanging down to her shoulders, I realized it was Lebanon. She was sitting in my chair in front of my fireplace! My mood sank to my feet. I walked over to the fireplace, retrieved *David Copperfield* from the bookshelf, and sat in a chair on the opposite side of the room without a word.

"Now, this is just silly, don't you think? There's enough room in front of the fire for both of us, you know. C'mon, don't be a dimwit. Bring your chair, you must be cold to the bone," Lebanon said, turning in her chair to look at me. Her quaint English accent reminded me of a Jane Austin novel turned into a film with modern vernacular. I reluctantly accepted her invitation, hoping she would be leaving soon. I took my chair to the fireplace, sat beside her, and immediately began to read my book with earnest. This time, *David Copperfield* was going to be different. He would not be mistreated by his stepfather, and his mother was not going to die. Mr. Micawber was not going to be an impecunious loser, and Mr. Dick was going to be in possession of all his mental faculties. Most importantly, Uriah Heep was never going to get the opportunity to implement any of his schemes. No, his constant handwringing was going to reveal the slimy character that he was, and David was going to notice it immediately. Yes, *David Copperfield* was going to be different this time. But his words to Agnes were going to remain exactly the same: "I have loved you all my life."

"The people in the hostel are talking about you, you know," Lebanon said suddenly without looking up from the magazine she was reading. I realized that I hadn't read a word all the time I was sitting next to her and was just staring at the page.

"So, what are they saying?" I finally managed to get out as nonchalantly as I possibly could.

She dropped her magazine upside down in her lap, drew her legs up underneath her, and turned sideways in her chair with her head resting against the backrest. "Oh, you know how it is with people. Everybody loves a good mystery, and for the moment, you are it. You never talk to anyone, and we hardly see you at all, except in the mornings when you're on your way to bed. Nobody is saying anything bad. Mostly everyone is just speculating about where you are from. So, let's put an end to the rumors and the mystery; tell me where you're from, Neil."

She knew my name. I'm sure I was visibly surprised. "How did you—"

"I peeked in the guest register. Hope you don't mind, but I was curious. Sadly, it didn't have anything about where you're from."

For a few moments, I was stunned. I closed my book, put another log on the fire, and said, "I'm from South Africa," as I sat back down.

"I'm Lebanon by the way," she said, extending her hand.

"Hi, I'm Neil, but you already know that, don't you," I said, taking her hand and giving it one decisive shake.

"So, what brings you to Inverness, Neil?"

It was clear that Lebanon wanted to have a conversation, and to be honest, it felt good to talk to someone for a change. "I got on a bus at Victoria station in London, and it brought me here."

"That's it? You didn't come for the whiskey or Loch Ness or the castles?"

"Well, until that day I didn't even know that Inverness existed. I simply walked into the station and bought a ticket for the first bus that was leaving. What brings you to Inverness?"

"Oh, it's such a long story, but I'll try and condense it for you." Lebanon began to talk animatedly. I was amazed at how easy she found it to talk to a complete stranger. Her mother had trained as a nurse in Lebanon and left her country to live in France. Her father was an English engineer who worked in Paris. The two of them met, fell in love, got married, and had one child—Lebanon. She grew up between Paris and London, and after school she wanted to become a model. I could imagine her as a model; she almost looked Mediterranean with her long, dark hair and almond skin. After the modeling hadn't worked out as she planned, her father sent her to university, where she had obtained a degree in economics only five months previously. Two days previously she had accepted a job as a bar lady at one of the local pubs in Inverness, and her shift ended at two in the mornings. That's how she ended up in my chair in front of my fireplace.

"Anyway, after Mom and Dad got married, they spent their honeymoon in Inverness. I grew up listening to stories about how beautiful it was here and how friendly the people were. I just had to see it for myself. So, that's my story. That's why I'm in Inverness."

She had talked for nearly half an hour, and the sudden quiet after she was finished was overwhelming. I opened my book again and pretended that I'd found the page I was looking for. But I didn't read; I just stared at the page again.

"Are you traveling alone?" she asked after several minutes.

"Why do you ask?"

"Well, it's just that most people travel in pairs. Just look at the people in the hostel. They are all paired up."

"Traveling alone is much easier. I can just pack my things one day and leave."

"So, what are you running away from?" She said it playfully without implying anything sinister, but her question infuriated me.

"Who says I'm running away from anything," I said sharply and almost offensively.

"You have that look in your eyes, Neil," she said running her fingers slowly through her hair. She seemed to not know exactly what to make of my display.

I didn't say anything after that. We were both silent.

"Well, I'm off the bed. Sleep well. It was nice meeting you," Lebanon said. Then she got up and walked out of the lounge.

Since reading that e-mail about Orphan's death, I'd begun to have the most horrible nightmares. Mostly they were about dead or dying orphans and children. Some nights my father would be among them and sometimes Zulu would be among them. Many nights I would wake up in a pool of sweat and scared to death.

I was in a bad mood the following day, and the shift at the salmon plant didn't help much either. I got back that morning exhausted, but strangely excited about the prospect that Lebanon might be in the lounge in front of the fireplace. I felt horrible for snapping at her the previous night.

I didn't go to the kitchen first, as I usually did, but peeked into the lounge to see if she was there. She had already pulled two chairs in front of the fireplace and a cup of coffee was on the floor next to mine. I walked over, sat down next to her, took my cup of coffee, and looked into the flames.

"You're back. How was your shift?" she asked, seeming to be just as excited as the previous night.

"It's not exactly a dream job but it pays well."

Lebanon smiled at me and continued reading her magazine. I threw more logs onto the fire and sat back down, sighing loudly.

"And what was that sigh for?" she asked.

"I'm sorry about last night," I blurted before I could think of how to put it a better way.

"What happened last night?"

"I'm sorry for snapping at you. I didn't mean to speak to you that way," I said, looking into the fire as if the flames could somehow help me with my apology.

"Look at me, Neil."

I turned my head and looked at her.

"You're forgiven. Now, let's go for a walk. I'm tired of reading," she said as she dropped her magazine on the floor next to her chair and stood up. I got up and followed her out of the lounge and to the front door.

"Where are we going?" I asked as I put on my heavy winter jacket.

"Does it really matter?" she asked, smiling playfully at me. "How much of Inverness have you actually seen?"

"I work in the evenings and sleep during the day, so I think it's safe to say I haven't seen anything yet."

"Well then, you're going to love this. Follow me." She flung open the door and led the way.

The streets were totally deserted. For all I knew, we were the only two people awake. We walked down the main street toward the river, turned left, walked up the hill, and climbed the steps leading to Inverness Castle. I remembered seeing it in the distance when I first got off the bus at the station. We walked around the east wall and came to a bench overlooking the river. Lebanon sat down and motioned me to sit.

"I come here a lot," she said when I finally sat down. "You should actually see it during the day. Sometimes I bring bread with me to feed the seagulls. I love to see how they glide down to peck the crumbs and crusts from the ground without landing. Seagulls are funny that way, you know; they hardly ever land when someone is feeding them. The locals don't actually encourage feeding the gulls, because they can become somewhat of a nuisance, but no one has ever told me to stop.

"I feel sorry for them; they are just looking for something to eat." She looked at me, as if to make sure I was following her. She pointed with her left hand to the river. "That is the river Ness. It goes all the way to the south and meets Loch Ness. You have heard of Loch Ness, haven't you? Some people believe there's an ancient monster lurking beneath the waters, but I think it is nonsense. Nevertheless, Inverness still attracts thousands of people each year, although tourism seems to die down during the winter months."

"Thank you for the coffee," I blurted, completely off the subject.

Lebanon spun her head toward me, looking confused for a couple of moments. "Oh, you mean the coffee in the lounge. It's nothing," she said almost shyly. "What made you think about the coffee now?"

"It's been a while since anyone made me a cup of coffee. You tend to notice these things when it actually happens again after a long time."

"It was just a cup of coffee, Neil, not a million pounds." She play-punched me on the shoulder.

"I know, but still, I noticed it." I said, looking at my feet.

"Wow, you really appreciate the small things, don't you?"

"Yeah, and I'd really appreciate something small to sit on. My butt is freezing."

Lebanon laughed loudly, as if nothing in the world was holding her back. The silence of that morning was ripped to pieces by her laughter. Then she said, "Let's get back to the hostel before you freeze your butt off then. Maybe I'll even make you another cup of coffee."

We walked back to the hostel, talking about the seagulls that she liked feeding. I was convinced that feeding them made her happier than anything in the world. Back inside, she made coffee, and we sat in front of the fireplace again.

"May I ask you something?" I asked as I threw the last log for the night onto the fire.

"Sure, what is it?"

"Why are you traveling alone? I've seen how the guys in the hostel look at you. Why don't you have a boyfriend?"

Lebanon turned in her seat again with her legs pulled up underneath her. "I had a boyfriend up until about six months ago. I was crazy about him at first. You know how it feels when you meet someone for the first time, and they sweep you off your feet? Well that was how it was for me with Greg. But I always seem to fall for guys who end up treating me like rubbish. I grew tired of his friends and their drinking.

"No matter how hard I try, I always seem to find the ones who don't deserve me. It's not easy to find a decent boyfriend in London, you know. That's part of the reason why I'm here. I've been single for six months now, and it was the best thing I could have done. I'll be in Inverness for another two months, and then I'm off to France to visit an aunt for a few weeks. After that, I'm going to Dubrovnik with a few friends. Daddy said I could have a mini gap year, but after Dubrovnik I have to find work. Serious work. A career. Not on his dole anymore."

She took another sip of her coffee. "Do you think it's vain of me to say that he didn't deserve me?"

"I don't think so."

"That's a safe answer, Neil. Don't give me that. I'm serious here. Tell me what you really think," she said sharply.

What did I really think? My thoughts were doing backflips. Lebanon was staring at me, waiting for an answer. "I don't know you, Lebanon." I said softly, looking at my feet again. "All I have to go on is two cups of coffee and a freezing geography lesson. Let's see, you love to feed birds, and you talk with an energy that I don't understand. You laugh with abandon, and you always sit with your legs drawn up underneath you. You like to play with your hair, you read fashion magazines instead of books, and you talked to me when no one else cared to do it. If this is all I have to go on, then I'll have to say no. No, he didn't deserve you. I don't know him or anything about him, but I feel sorry for him."

I looked up from my feet to find Lebanon looking at me as if I were from another planet. She seemed amazed, almost stunned—as if the challenge to answer her truthfully was completely met and won.

There was silence for a few moments. I continued drinking my coffee, not wanting to hold her gaze.

"I don't get you, you know," she said. "You don't say much, but just now, you took my breath away. You never seem to look at me. You're always looking at your feet or looking into the flames, and yet you notice small things. Why don't you ever look at me?"

"I think I've seen too much, and for the moment I'm happy with just looking at my feet," I said, doing my utmost best to look at her and not my feet or the fire or the cup of coffee in my hands.

"You don't look at me, but you see me, don't you?" she said softly, resting her head against the backrest of her chair.

"I think so."

"Are you a Christian, Neil?"

Lebanon's question startled me, but I decided to answer her truthfully. "I think I nearly was one once."

"What happened?"

"It's a long story. Why do you ask?"

"Some of us are going to church on Sunday, and I was wondering if you wanted to join us."

"I work on Sundays. I take it you're a Christian?"

"I'm a Catholic girl. But don't believe a word they say about Catholic girls," she said with a chuckle.

"Like what? You're the first Catholic person I know."

"Really? Never mind then." She seemed pleased that I didn't understand what she meant. (Today I believe she was referring to the stereotype that Catholic women are sexually frustrated and repressed.)

This was how Lebanon and I spent our mornings. Most mornings we would just sit in front of the fireplace talking or reading. Every morning when I got back to the hostel, there was a cup of coffee waiting for me next to my chair. Some mornings, when we felt brave enough, we went for walks in the deserted and cold streets of Inverness. I never told her anything about the Air Force or my life before I came to the United Kingdom, and Lebanon, being the person she was, never asked. Perhaps she sensed that I didn't want to talk about it.

We were reading one morning when Lebanon suddenly said, "Are you going to take a day off anytime soon? You've been working straight through for nearly three weeks now."

"I asked for a day off this Sunday. I was thinking that you could show me how you feed the seagulls."

"You sneaky bastard!" She laughed and play-punched me on the shoulder. "I would very much like to show you." She continued reading her magazine, and she was visibly happy.

I had planned to sleep late that Sunday morning, but at nine, Lebanon burst into my room with a cup of coffee. I protested for a while, arguing that the seagulls would still be there at eleven, but she wouldn't take no for an answer. After I had taken a shower, I went to the lounge and found Lebanon sitting with the two French girls. She introduced me to them, and after another cup of coffee, she and I left. We walked out of the hostel and down the main street toward a parked car.

"Whose car is this?" I asked.

"I rented it this morning while you were still sleeping."

"What about the seagulls? Where are we going?"

"Well, I thought that we'd do what tourists normally do when they come to Scotland. We're going to see castles and taste whiskey," She seemed almost proud of herself. "And besides, the seagulls aren't going anywhere. We can feed them some other time. Get into the car, Neil. You're going to love this."

I was speechless and got into the car slightly stunned.

"So, where do you want to go first?" she asked.

"I don't know. You should have told me about this so I could've prepared or something."

"Where's the fun in that? C'mon, Neil, it's an amazing day. We have a car for twenty-four hours, we're in the Highlands of Scotland, and our shifts start tomorrow evening at five."

"Okay, let's just drive then. Start the car and just drive. We are bound to come across something interesting." This time I was the one who was visibly happy.

We drove around in the Highlands the rest of that day, stopping at any place that looked even remotely interesting. Our first stop was at Urquhart Castle on the western bank of Loch Ness. There wasn't much left of the castle—only a few walls and stones—but the visitor's center had lots of interesting information about its origin and its original owners. According to them, the castle was more than 1,200 years old. I couldn't comprehend such history.

After walking among the ruins for a couple of minutes and taking a lot of pictures, we got back into the car and drove to Fort William at the southern tip of Loch Lochy. I don't think any place is as beautiful as the Highlands of Scotland in autumn. Every leaf on every tree had turned to deep, burnished browns, reds, and yellows. The gray rocks of Ben Nevis seemed to be whispering to everything around them, "We have seen and know all." The rolling green glens of Scotland are forever burned into my mind. Time goes by slower there. God took his time and gave special attention the day he created the Highlands. Angels go there to relax.

At about noon, we stopped at a village and had lunch in one of the local pubs. That was the first time I'd had the opportunity to taste the local beer. Hideous! Lebanon was ecstatic though. She loved showing me the places and driving me around as if she was my personal tour guide for the day.

Since my arrival in the UK, I had been working constantly, except between jobs at the hostel in London, and it felt good to finally get out and see the things that other people talked about so much. Though I still had nightmares and I still had an unpredictable temper, driving around that day with no idea where we were going brought me very close to happiness. That day made everything else seem so distant and trivial.

We drove to a distillery to taste some of the finest whiskeys in the world. We paid thirty pounds each for a guided tour, which ended in the tasting room where barrels and barrels of whiskey stood waiting. We started with a relatively young whiskey of five years. At year forty-five, Lebanon and I decided to call it quits. Maybe we were a little tipsy, but neither of us looked forward to driving back to Inverness, so we decided that we would drive back to Loch Ness to see if we could get a room in one of the many guesthouses we'd seen on our way to Fort William.

As luck would have it, we found a room in the first guesthouse we enquired at and after settling things with the owner and putting our things in our room, we drove to the village to buy toothbrushes and toothpaste. I dropped Lebanon at a mini-market and drove to a gas station to fill the car and when I drove back to pick her up, she was waiting in front of the mini-market with two grocery bags.

"I thought you were going to get toothbrushes and toothpaste," I said as she got into the car.

"I did, but I also bought myself a T-shirt and shorts, and a long, cotton trouser with drawstrings for you."

"What are those for?"

"To sleep in, dimwit." She added casually, "Oh, and I also bought a bottle of red wine."

When we got back to the guesthouse, the owner had already started a fire in our fireplace and had placed fresh towels on the beds. It felt like such a perfect day. The air was crisp and clear and cold and refreshing. We drank red wine and sat in front of the fire, recalling every single village we'd driven through and every single whiskey we'd tasted. For just a while, the fish packing became a faint memory. For just a while, she wasn't a bar lady at a pub.

When Lebanon took a shower, I switched on the TV to see if there was any news about South Africa, but every channel I changed to only had something about the war in Iraq. I hated war, so I switched it off again and sat in front of the window. Loch Ness sparkled in the distance, and the cool evening breeze felt refreshing after the heat of the fire. I had many thoughts at that point, but I couldn't single out one of them. So I simply let my mind drift from one to the other. The taste of the red wine in my mouth was soothing.

She came out of the shower in a cloud of steam. She wore the T-shirt and shorts from the mini-market with a towel wrapped around her head, and she was humming a song softly. *She is such a woman,* I thought. I pretended not to look at her, feeling uneasy with how comfortable she was with my presence. *How do women around the world know how to do that with a towel around their heads?* I thought as she unwrapped it and started to dry her hair with it. She poured herself another glass of wine and came to sit next to me on the sofa I had pulled in front of the window.

"The guest house is so much better than the hostel, don't you think?" she said as she finally got comfortable.

"Yeah, and it's more expensive too," I said, knowing that the room had cost me nearly two hundred pounds for the night. I thought it only fair that I pay for our room, as she was the one who rented the car.

"Go on, go take a shower. It's so lovely not having to share a shower with ten other people. I'll keep your seat for you."

The bathroom had a "power-shower"—a device in the shower that delivered multiple jets of steaming hot water. Lebanon was right; it felt unbelievably good. I finally came out of the bathroom in an even bigger cloud of steam. The cold air in the room from the open window gave me goose bumps, but it was refreshing. Lebanon was still sitting in front of the window, sipping her wine and looking at Loch Ness in the distance, which was by then bathed in moonlight.

We talked in front of the window for a long time and finally moved to the fireplace when it became too cold. We didn't have any books, so we talked as if nothing in the world was more important. Eventually we went to bed, talking with the lights off and the fire crackling in the fireplace. I can't actually recall the process of falling asleep.

I woke up at about two in the morning, wet with sweat and with my heart pounding. I had had another one of those horrible nightmares and was upset. I got up as quietly as I could, opened the window, and sat on the sofa, allowing the night breeze to cool my wet skin. I was so tired of feeling helpless and angry and not knowing what to do.

"What's wrong, Neil?" Lebanon asked suddenly from her bed.

"Nothing. I'll be fine in a moment. I didn't mean to wake you. Go back to sleep."

I sat in front of that window, completely exhausted, not from lack of sleep, but from the repetition of it all.

Suddenly Lebanon was behind me. "Are you sure you're all right?"

"I said I'm fine, okay!" I shouted, but immediately felt horrible for talking to her that way. I sighed deeply. "I'm sorry, Lebanon. I didn't mean to snap at you. I'm just tired, that's all."

Lebanon didn't say a word. Perhaps she was even a little afraid of me. I heard her sit down on the bed behind me. My back was turned to her as I sat on the sofa.

"I don't know if I can do this anymore, Lebanon. I'm tired of being lonely and angry all the time. I'm tired of waking up in the middle of the night scared to death."

"Would you like to pray with me?" she asked softly.

"I'd rather not."

"Why not?"

"I don't think God cares," I said as casually as I could.

"Don't be silly. Of course God cares."

*How dare she? How dare she so casually come to the defense of a God I didn't know?* I was furious in an instant and jumped to my feet.

"That's bullshit, Lebanon! God does not care!" I was shouting now and looked directly at her as she sat on the bed.

"Why do you say that, Neil? God loves you."

"That's something people say when they don't understand things. God loves you! Those three words are supposed to make everything better, right? Well, I'm sorry, it doesn't! God doesn't care, Lebanon, and if he does care, then I will just have to accept that God doesn't care about *me*!" I was pacing up and down in front of the sofa. "Do you want to hear something funny? I have two degrees, but I think I know more about history, philosophy, evolution, and science! I put so much effort into trying to understand how God works, but I am still left with nothing. I'm angry with God because he doesn't seem to want me, and I want him to want me. Is that so wrong? I'm different, Lebanon. I'm kinda quiet, even shy. I can lose myself in a painting or a beautiful poem. Did you see the sunset yesterday when we drove back from Fort William? I loved it! I was lost in it! That's how I want God to want me. Yes, he wants all of humanity, I get it! But what about *me*? All I get to have is an intimate knowledge of death and pain!"

"What really happened, Neil? Why are you so angry?" she asked softly from the bed.

"Because—" I caught myself. "Never mind."

"You can trust me, Neil," she said almost pleadingly.

"Because I think I'm responsible for my father's death, okay! I didn't return his call the night before he killed himself. Do you have any idea what that feels like? What kind of son does that? What kind of son ignores his father's phone call? How am I supposed to get over that? How am I supposed to tell my family that? They'll hate me! I hate myself!"

Lebanon didn't say a word. She just sat on the bed and looked at me.

"I served in the Air Force with a Zulu a couple of months ago. He just couldn't shut up about Jesus. Despite the fact that he had every reason to hate a silly white man like me, he was kind to me. He was my friend. Ask me what happened to him?"

Lebanon was quiet.

"Ask me what happened to him, dammit!" I shouted.

She dropped her eyes and looked at her hands. "What happened to him?"

"He was killed for his shoes and his wallet. I loved him! I wanted to be like him! But instead he ended up dead before I could thank him for his kindness and his friendship!"

Lebanon didn't move. She seemed uneasy with all my shouting, ranting, and raving.

"After he died, I wanted to do something special in his memory and eventually decided to pledge money for the care of war orphans in Burundi. Later, for some reason I still don't understand, I started to send e-mails as well. And then four weeks ago, I get an e-mail from some nun telling me that the orphan she read my e-mails to died of AIDS. But that's not the sad part! The sad part is that the poor girl thought the letters were written by Jesus.

"Did you hear what I just said? Instead of Jesus being in her life in a real way, she ended up thinking that I was Jesus! Why doesn't God do something? Why does he leave it up to us to try to make a difference? There are forty five million orphans in Africa alone! That's like the entire population of a small country! Thousands of them die every day, and God doesn't do a thing! Why doesn't he just end it all?"

"It will, you know," she said softly.

"Will what?"

"End. It's just a question of time, Neil."

"And what are we supposed to do in the meantime?"

"Pray. Be kind to others. Have faith."

"Why doesn't God want me, Lebanon?" I asked desperately.

"In many ways you are closer to God now than you realize, Neil."

"How do you figure?"

"Do you know the parable about the lost sheep? You're that lost sheep, Neil. God is looking for you this very moment."

"Why doesn't he find me then? I can't imagine that I'm that difficult to find! Besides, I'm the one looking for him. Why should I be the one to initiate if I am so important to him?

"God always initiates, Neil. He never gives up. And he will find you. I promise you."

I didn't have anything else to say. I sank down on the sofa and allowed my heartbeat to slow down. Where did she find the courage to do what she did next? Where did she find the courage to approach an enraged man? She got up from the bed and walked to the front of the sofa, took me by the hand, and led me back to the bed, where she made me sit next to her. Then she took my head and laid it in her lap. "You're going to have to stop running at some point, Neil," she said running her fingers slowly through my hair. "The world isn't big enough."

Perhaps it was the feeling of the cold air against my skin. Maybe it was the warmth of Lebanon's lap, her hands in my hair, or the comfort she gave me, but at that moment the volcano I had been keeping quiet inside me for so long erupted. I was twenty-six years old, but I cried like a baby. I sobbed violently and loudly, shaking the bed along with Lebanon as I did so.

For the first time since my father's death nearly five years earlier I grieved for him. I grieved for not returning his call. I grieved for Zulu and for never apologizing to him for what white people did to him, his parents, and his grandparents. I grieved for a nameless and faceless orphan who wanted to play with horses.

I calmed down after a while, feeling utterly embarrassed for crying in front of her. She never said a word but kept running her fingers slowly through my hair. I got up after lying quiet for a while longer, went to the bathroom, splashed water on my face, and looked at my reflection in the mirror. Where did my thoughts go then? I was six thousand miles away from home and in the next room was a woman who had just sparked something inside me I could not describe. What was that infinitesimal glimmer? What feeling had approached me from afar?

I looked at my reflection in the mirror and thought about a quote from Bernard Baruch I once used in high school during a debate in English class.[1] He told the story of a man sentenced to death who obtained a reprieve by assuring the king he would teach his majesty's horse to fly within the year. His condition was that if he didn't succeed, he would be put to death at the end of the year. "Within a year," the man explained later, "the king may die, or I may die, or the horse may die. Furthermore, in a year, who knows? Maybe the horse will learn to fly."

Why did I think of that story then, there in the bathroom with puffy eyes and water dripping from my scruffy beard? What is it that this story speaks of? And then it became clear to me. It was hope. Hope against all odds. Hope when things are hopeless. Hope that whatever Lebanon had begun inside me would one day reach maturity. Hope that one day the darkness and pain would leave me forever. Hope that God would never give up and that he would find me.

When I came out of the bathroom, I found Lebanon still sitting in the same position on the bed. I sat down next to her and sighed loudly and deeply, and said, "I'm sorry. I didn't mean for that to happen."

"Maybe it needed to happen" was all she said. I thought perhaps she was right.

We were still awake when the sun started to rise, and we ended up on the sofa, looking out of the window at the impending dawn and the sunrise that would soon follow. She was so beautiful then. She looked so radiant. Neither of us said a word. Sometimes words aren't needed. She looked out over Loch Ness, and I looked at her. She seemed so at peace. She seemed so content. She was in a place where nothing mattered. I wanted to be there too.

We never spoke about that night in the guesthouse again, but we continued as we always did. Nearly every morning there was a cup of coffee on the floor next to my chair in front of the fireplace. Some mornings we spent reading while others we would talk about anything. And we still went for walks some mornings in the cold and deserted streets of Inverness. Eventually we even got around to feeding the

---

[1] Bernard Mannes Baruch (August 19, 1870-June 20, 1965) was an American financier, stock-market speculator, statesman, and political consultant. After his success in business, he devoted his time to advising US presidents Woodrow Wilson and Franklin D. Roosevelt on economic matters.

seagulls. It's true what she said: they hardly ever land when someone is feeding them.

In some way I became less guarded with Lebanon. I didn't look at my feet as much but instead looked at her. Sometimes I even turned sideways in my chair to listen to her as she talked. I don't recall the exact moment we became friends. Maybe we were friends the moment I found her in my chair in front of "my" fireplace that morning. Maybe we became friends when she gave me a freezing geography lesson. Maybe we became friends when she showed me the Highlands of Scotland. Or maybe we became friends when, in a moment of weakness, I showed her my heart and cried on her lap.

Time and weeks went by, and the time for Lebanon to leave Inverness grew closer and closer. We had talked about it and agreed that I would help her carry her things to the station after we had spent one more morning in front of the fireplace. I wasn't looking forward to saying good-bye to her that Sunday.

I came home that morning knowing that it would be our last morning together. I walked into the lounge, saw that she wasn't there yet, and went to the kitchen to make two cups of coffee. I took both cups to the fireplace, set hers on the floor next to her chair, and saw an envelope in mine. I picked it up and read my name on the front. I opened it and started to read:

> My dearest Neil,
>
> I hope you can forgive me for leaving this way, but I can't stand the thought of saying goodbye to you. I'm taking the train to London after you leave for your shift. Please don't be angry with me, Neil. I think a part of me is afraid that you will ask me to stay, because I know that I will stay in a heartbeat. I think an even bigger part of me is afraid that you won't ask (girls are weird aren't they?). The thing is—I have fallen in love with you.
>
> I have to be honest—I kinda liked you the first time I saw you, you know. You with your quiet confidence and air of mystery. I am 24 years old, and over the years I

have grown used to the way men look at me. At times it is very flattering and sometimes it infuriates me, but never before has a man really seen me for who I am. Until you came along and without any effort at all, you seemed to see me without even looking at me. Do you remember that morning in the guesthouse when we sat on the sofa, waiting for the sun to rise? I pretended not to notice, but you were looking at me then. God, I felt so beautiful that morning!

Every woman has a place deep inside her heart that few people ever reach. Perhaps it's the place where all desires and secrets are kept. You occupy that place in my heart now Neil. I will get married one day, and maybe I'll even have children, but that place in my heart can never belong to anyone else. You will live there forever.

Please understand Neil. This is the most difficult thing I have ever had to do. If I stay, I will only get in the way. I've prayed about this for a long time and I know that I cannot help you find God—God will find you on his own. I do not want to get in the way of that. Some things are more important than a woman's heart.

Always remember that things happen when they need to happen—even the bad things, and everything happens for a reason. There's a reason why you got on that bus in London that day. There's a reason why it brought you to Inverness. There's a reason why we ended up in front of the same fireplace, and there's a reason why we became so "close" in such a short period of time. I don't know what that reason is, but I know that God knows.

I know we haven't spoken about that night in the guesthouse again, but I would like to say something about it now. I have a theory about the letters that little girl received. You said that she thought they were written by Jesus. Well, I think I agree with her. Jesus wrote those letters Neil, not you. He just needed someone to type them. I don't know what it feels like to lose a parent, but I do know what it feels like to lose a friend—it's never an easy thing. The evil in this world isn't God's fault Neil. He hates it just like you do. His heart is also broken—just like yours.

You were always thanking me for small things. Allow me now to thank you. Thank you for sharing the fireplace with me. Thank you for walking with me in the cold morning hours. Thank you for feeding the seagulls with me. Thank you for exploring the Highlands with me. Thank you for sharing your tears with me. Thank you for making me feel so beautiful. Thank you for always treating me like a lady.

Inside the envelope you will find a Saint Christopher's pendant. Daddy gave it to me on my eighteenth birthday and made me promise that I would give it away someday (it's a Catholic thing). Saint Christopher is the patron saint of travelers. I know you're not Catholic, but I am. Promise me that you will wear it around your neck and that you will give it away someday.

I pray with all my heart that God finds you in the way you want him to. I will never forget you . . .

All my love,

Lebanon

And just like that, Lebanon was gone—like a whirlwind or like lightning.

I remained in Inverness a while longer, and I still sat in front of the fireplace. I still went for walks in the cold morning hours, and I still fed the seagulls. But it just wasn't the same. My thoughts would constantly return to her seagulls and her God-talk that night in the guesthouse.

# 11

## EIFFEL

*Life is a series of natural and spontaneous changes. Don't resist them—that only creates sorrow. Let reality be reality. Let things flow naturally forward in whatever way they like.*

—LAO TZU

I grew tired of smelling of fish every day and eventually left Inverness after I found a job at a livestock auction center in Inverurie near Aberdeen on the east coast of Scotland. I carried Lebanon's letter in my back pocket and read it whenever I had time or during a break.

I enjoyed working with live animals (as opposed to dead fish). Cattle would chew cud all day long and sheep would do what they do best—bleat. I seemed to be better with animals than I was with humans. I exchanged the fireplace in the hostel for a gas heater in a mobile cabin, but Lebanon's seagulls followed me (actually, Aberdeen had its own seagulls, but I liked the thought of her seagulls following me).

On days off, the people I worked with and I would drive to Aberdeen and walk around looking for something to buy, which usually included whiskey—the only effective way to keep warm in a country that was wet and cold.

After about a month in Inverurie, I found a job on a cattle farm in North Hampton near the village of Yelvertoft, just twenty miles from Rugby. Another mobile cabin, another gas heater, more snow. I worked with an Aussie from Sydney who had the uncanny ability to finish my sentences for me, and although he was human, I seemed to get along with him just fine (he didn't chew cud, and he didn't bleat). We took turns cooking, and the farmer was kind enough to supply us with all the steaks we needed. Only a South African and an Aussie would venture outside and brave freezing weather to barbecue a couple of steaks in a snowstorm. The farmer must have thought we were crazy.

Our days consisted of cleaning the cattle pens, putting down straw, feeding the bulls and cows, and tending to the calves. Then, one day, the farmer announced that we would be "preg testing" the following day. I didn't know what preg testing was, but Aussie didn't look too pleased.

"Great! We'll be covered in cow sh*t from head to toe." Seeing the puzzled look on my face, he explained what preg testing was in graphic detail—testing cows for pregnancy.

"Stick my arm up where?!" I exclaimed.

"Yup, the cows are gonna give us funny looks for days."

I didn't look forward to violating cows with my arm, and Aussie was right—we were covered in cow pooh, and my imagination convinced me that the cows were really looking at us in a funny way.

Leaving Yelvertoft, I decided to meet up with two friends. They were a set of twins who served in the Air Force with me. We'd completed the officer formative course and attended the military academy together. They had resigned from the Air Force when I did, and I felt responsible for their decision. I didn't want them to blame me if things didn't turn out well. Now one is a programmer and the other works as an IT manager. I suppose things worked out well in the end for both of them. They are the only two people other than my family I have known for more than twelve years; they are good friends.

At the time, the twins were working at a factory in Hampshire that produced cement garden "objects." I found a job at the same factory (actually the twins found the job for me), but I quickly missed working on a farm. There was just something about working outside that soothed me. When the factory job started to get too predictable (can a factory job be any different?), I called the agent in London and asked for a job for three people on a farm. As luck would have it, there was a farm park in St. Albans who needed three workers.

Willows Farm Park was nothing more than a glorified petting zoo. Parents would bring their children to look at and feed the animals—everything from rabbits and guinea pigs to cattle and goats. The farm also had two main attractions: a ride on a trailer attached to a tractor and a boat ride on the lake. Although work on the farm park wasn't rocket science either, at least I was with friends who spoke my language.

I have never told them anything about myself and I suppose over the years, they've made peace with the fact that Dave (my military nickname) keeps to himself mostly. I didn't tell them how my father died (although I knew them when he was still alive). I've never told them about Zulu or Orphan or Lebanon, and I've certainly never told them that I think God doesn't seem to care about me or that I wanted him to send me a letter.

I suppose that when my friends read this book, things will make more sense and will fall into place. They'll know why I had such a bad temper at the academy and they'll understand why I always seemed to be asleep. (I was awake at night trying to prove the existence of God or finding his true identity by reading books.)

The academy yearbook of 2000 is a case in point. All students were required to supply a personal motto to include in the yearbook along with their photos. I was awake and present for the photos, but the day we had to supply our personal mottos, I was tucked away in La-La Land. Someone thought it would be a good idea to supply my motto for me:

Lieutenant Neil S. Davies
Motto:
"Wake me up before you go-go."

The twins went home for a month, and only one twin came back. (The other one decided to stay in South Africa and find meaningful employment. The twins are now just Twin.)

Twin and I grew tired of pleasing children all day and decided to call the agent in London for another job. Three weeks later, Twin and I headed for South Yorkshire to work on Roche Abbey farm near the village of Maltby. It was the start of the harvest season, a very busy time for crop farmers all over the world, and workers (tractor drivers) were in high demand. The farmer allowed us to stay in a four-bedroom cottage on the farm—a far cry from the mobile cabins I had grown used to. It had a television, washing machine, stove, double beds, toaster and, to my delight, a power shower.

I still carried Lebanon's letter in my back pocket, only to be read during lunch times when I gave the tractor (and myself) a break by parking on the side of the field I had to plough (or cultivate or disk or subsoil). By this time, I had grown increasingly restless. God exists. I believed it. But I didn't know what faith felt like or what it meant to have a personal relationship with him. *God doesn't want me,* I thought. And getting a letter from him was a ridiculous thought (but a sincere one). *If God is really looking for me, how will I know that I am 'found'?*

My birthday was coming up, and Twin and I decided to go to Paris for three days. We made arrangements with the farmer, obtained visas, booked a room in a hotel, and flew to Paris from Manchester Airport a few weeks later. I think I knew that I would be returning to South Africa before we went to Paris. I was convinced that God was not looking for me and just wanted to continue with my life as best I could. God belonged to other people—friends and family—but not to me. Yes, I knew that I would return to South Africa before we went to Paris.

We took a taxi from Charles de Gaulle Airport to Hotel Montholon on Rue de Montholon, walking distance from La Poissoniere Metro Station. Those three days were truly amazing, and we did what normal tourists do: we explored. We climbed the 284 steps of the Arc de Triomphe; drank red wine and had lunch at Café Vesuvio on Avenue des Champs-Elysees; visited the Louvre and saw the Mona Lisa; and went to the top of the Eiffel Tower on the night of my birthday. I will never forget that night. *Go home and get busy with life,* I told myself. *God doesn't want you.* And that's precisely what I did.

# 12

## I Am Found

*Life is what happens while*
*you are busy making other plans.*

—JOHN LENNON

It is here that I would like to bite my thumb at my eleventh-grade English Literature teacher (with respect of course). He always told me that my sentences were too short, that my thoughts were all over the place, and that I wrote in a staccato fashion. He was right, and as a tribute to him, I will now attempt to explain what it means to get busy with life in true staccato fashion (this chapter describes nearly three years of my life after returning to South Africa).

I landed a job as magazine editor and kept myself busy with magazine proof pages, faxes, letters, articles from contributors, photo shoots, page layouts, page designs, meetings, interviews, e-mails, deadlines, fights, stress, coffee, cigarettes, telephone calls, magazine printers, magazine competitions, magazine prizes, complaints, winners, losers.

I bought a BMW; ordered a motorcycle manual from Japan; took my motorcycle apart; put my motorcycle back together; went for proper horse-riding lessons; sold the BMW; went for guitar lessons; developed stomach ulcers; struggled with insomnia; corresponded with an American soldier who fought in Iraq; started writing scripts for corporate videos; kept clients happy; took my motorcycle apart again; smoked like a chimney; bought my own saddle; bought another drum set; got a girlfriend; changed jobs; started to write scripts for television; broke up with the girlfriend . . .

I was going through my things one night when I found Lebanon's letter and the e-mail about Orphan's death in a box marked "UK" under my bed. The last time I'd read Lebanon's letter was the night when Twin and I went back to our hotel after seeing Paris from the Eiffel Tower. Reading her letter again upset me. *Why doesn't God find me like Lebanon promised?*

Later that night I was involved in a serious motorcycle accident. A car skipped a traffic light, and when I slammed the Harley-Davidson into it, I didn't have any profound experiences other than flying through the air and landing in the road with a dull thud. I didn't see my life flash before my eyes. I didn't call God's name when I lay broken and in pain in a hospital bed, begging the nurses for morphine. I didn't pray in anguish when the doctor told me that the chances of me ever fathering children were very slim. I did nothing of the sort, but *getting busy with life* came to an abrupt end. I had sustained two broken ribs, a fractured pelvis, a broken collar bone, and hairline fractures in both of my wrists and my right foot. The pain was excruciating.

I underwent two surgeries—one for internal bleeding in a place I will rather not mention (denting the fuel tank with that part of my anatomy is something I will avoid in future), and another to insert seven surgical screws in my collar bone, which was badly broken. After about a week, I was sent home with "Try not to walk too much for a while." How could I? Walking with a broken pelvis and a messed-up foot isn't easy. Breathing with two broken ribs isn't easy. Opening a bottle or making coffee with cracked wrists isn't easy.

All I could really do effectively was watch television and read. I asked my mother to bring me a couple of books, and, being a crafty woman, she brought only the books she wanted me to read. The first book I read was C. S. Lewis's account of how God found him. Lewis said that God hunted him relentlessly. I was jealous of him. God wasn't hunting me. Later I started reading at least three books at a time—one in the living room, one in my room, and one in the bathroom. (I found that when I eventually moved, I tended to stay in one place for a while, as getting there took a lot of effort.)

I was on the porch one day (after taking about ten minutes to get there), drinking coffee, smoking a cigarette, and hating that I found it so difficult to quit smoking. Children were playing in the sandpit in front of the house, when I suddenly thought about Orphan again. She believed that Jesus wrote her letters once a month. A thought occurred to me then: *If I were God, how would I reach someone like me?* It was a casual thought, and I didn't expect that it would amount to much, but words not my own and feelings I can't describe welled up from deep inside me, and it was impossible to stop. It was only then that my life flashed before my eyes.

> If I were God, how would I reach someone like me? Well, I would poke him. I would poke him like an incessant Facebook friend. Considering his personality and how as a young boy he couldn't wait to go home after school so he could attack a suspicious British-looking shrub as a Zulu warrior, I would poke him with a gigantic Zulu who has the complete inability to shut up about me; a Zulu who would become the only friend to know his deepest secrets; a black South African who will never make him feel guilty for the history of a country they share, because I know he experiences guilt far too easily.
>
> Given how he reacts to a sunset, and how he keeps quiet when it happens because he doesn't want to miss it, I will poke him with sunset after sunset after sunset. I will poke him with a crazed and angry horse so that he wouldn't feel like such a failure because he didn't react to his father's voicemail. At least in some way he will feel that he helped another living thing, a horse, come to terms with and let go of its anger.
>
> Considering how easily he sees the romantic in everything, I will poke him with a semi-sober fisherman who tells him about the connection between mermaids and love so that he can get over a girl who broke his heart. I will poke him with a moving e-mail about an

orphan who couldn't wait to play with horses, even if it meant that she had to die.

Knowing that Khalil's Selma has mesmerized him so since he was sixteen years old, I will poke him with a girl in Scotland who will forever be that for him. Whenever he thinks about Khalil and Selma, Lebanon's face will appear in his mind so clearly it will be as if he saw her only yesterday. She would change his solitude in the Highlands of Scotland into happy moments and fill the silence of his nights in front of the fireplace with the music of her voice. I will even give him the letter he asked for so casually one night in Aberdeen, knowing that while he asked for it, it was already in his back pocket—a letter written by a half-Lebanese girl.

Yes, I will poke him. That's how I will reach him. I will poke him like an incessant Facebook friend, and he will know that he is mine and that he is found.

Something else happened next. It began slowly at first: an infinitesimal feeling in the pit of my stomach. It grew ever so slightly and filled every inch of my being. But it kept growing and filled my immediate surroundings—the couch I was sitting on, the porch, my house—and then it grew some more. It enveloped the children playing in the sandpit, the trees behind them, the neighbor's dog. It reached to the sky and kept on growing and pulled my soul along with it. It was everywhere in mere moments.

How will I ever find the words to describe that feeling? Human language is so limiting. Words are nothing more than placeholders for things and actions and concepts. When I say the word *trash can*, an image pops into my head of a can filled with garbage. Other people have images of the kitchen trash can or even a dumpster, but the visual queue remains intact: an object we put trash in.

With abstract concepts, though, things become a little more complicated. Words like *love*, *compassion*, *morality*, *good*, and *bad* conjure up different things for different people. The only word I have at my disposal to describe the feeling that emanated from within me, left my body, and entered the universe, is gratitude. That is what I felt—an immense, uncontrollable gratitude that touched everything around me.

I sighed deeply and said, "I am found." I said it as a matter of fact, not as a request or a statement of hope. It was a fact. I thought about that night in the guesthouse in Scotland when I splashed water on my face after crying like a baby on Lebanon's lap. The glimmer of hope I saw that night—hope against all odds, hope when things are hopeless—had come to fruition. I was, at long last, found. The darkness and pain that had been part of my heart for so long evaporated into nothingness. A heart filled with gratitude had evicted them.

I understood something then: we are loved—all of us. Loved. And there is nothing that can ever remove us from that love. Love is what sets everything in motion, and to be alive in this universe is to be the object of that motion. I understood that faith and spirituality are a matter of autobiography—the story of your own life—and that is how God becomes personal. That is how he becomes *my* God and not just the God we hear of in church or the God who is a mere spectator of the happenings here on Earth. He is intimately and sincerely involved in everything, not by obligation but by uninhibited, uncontrolled, fervent, passionate, and inexplicable love. I am loved. You are loved. We are all loved!

I spent a long while on the porch, drinking in the feeling that grew within my chest. I didn't want to remove myself from that moment. I experienced a peace that I had never felt before, but I knew that I had a life to live—a life that would be different from the one I had lived before. I got up from the couch and, minding my many broken bones, made my way slowly to my room. I sat at my desk, booted up my computer, and wrote the first few words of the first sentence of this book: "I thought about God for a very long time."

I didn't know that I was writing a book then, but the first sentence turned into a paragraph and then the paragraph turned into a page and then the page turned into a chapter and then another chapter. I didn't know what I was going to do with it once I was done, but I knew that a plan would develop as time went by.

* * *

**January 2012**

A few years have passed. I have moved to the United States where I work—yes, you guessed it—work on a farm in North Dakota. I work for a father-and-son outfit in Griggs County that farms about nine thousand acres, raising wheat, soybeans, and corn. I can't help but smile as I write this. Once upon a time I was an intelligence officer in the South African Air Force. I have traveled to England and Scotland and seen the lights of Paris from the top of the Eiffel Tower. And I am a qualified IT professional. But there is just something about life on a farm that I find very satisfying. (Note to self: (1) learn how to weld; (2) become more familiar with diesel engines, and (3) quit smoking, you idiot!).

While Mark and Deanne (the father of the father-and-son outfit and his wife) are away on a cruise to the Caribbean, I am taking care of their pets. Scratch (the cat) is lying right on top of my feet. Somehow, with her little cat brain, she has figured out that I like it when my feet are warm while I write. I think my rhythmic typing puts her to sleep.

Dirty Dog (the farm dog) is snoring up a storm on the couch. She's an old dog—totally deaf and, I suspect, partially blind. The local weather service has just issued a winter storm warning for a number of counties, including mine, and as I look out the window I see that it has started to snow. On days like this, I miss Africa. On days like this, my life flashes before my eyes, and I send a prayer into the universe:

> Lebanon, I want you to know what an impact you had on my life. You were patient and understanding. You were the best part of my day. Thank you for writing me a letter when you left. You will never know how much it meant to me. That letter made all the difference. I have misplaced it in the meantime, but I read it so many times that I know it by heart. I can still hear you laughing. I can still see your face.
>
> In 2008 I finally gave your necklace to someone else and made them promise that they will give it away when they feel the time is right. I bought myself another one, because without it around my neck, I feel naked. Perhaps

as time goes by, your necklace will make its way back to England and perhaps even to Scotland, where it belongs.

If you have made any mistakes since the last time we saw each other, I want you to please forget about it. God loves you. He loves us all, but I am certain that you are one of his favorites. Whenever I drink a cup of coffee, I think of you. Whenever I see or hear a seagull, I think of you. In my mind I see you now as a wife and loving mother. I pray that you are happy and fulfilled.

Zulu, you were my best friend. I regret that I never told you how important you were to me. I recall how much we suffered together during basic military training. I recall how you picked me up when I would face-plant in the dirt because of exhaustion. You allowed me to drink from your canteen when the water in mine was drained. You shared your food with me. You literally carried my load (my backpack) when I couldn't walk another step.

I became an officer while you remained an enlisted man, but you will always be the General of my life. You were my superior. I should have been the one to salute you. You were black and I am white, but we were friends regardless. Thank you for being such a true and honest friend.

I understand now that I am not my skin color. I am not my body, and I am not my gender. I am the ghost in my body-machine. In creating you, God revealed his perfection. I miss you. Next time we meet, I will have an eternity to be a better friend.

Orphan, I never knew you. I don't know what you looked like or even what your name was. I sent you e-mails and money once a month in memory of a dear

> friend. He was the bravest man I knew. In my mind you will always be six years old. Perhaps you have seen and ridden a horse in the meantime. Were you impressed? I can't wait to meet you. I have so much to tell you.
>
> Amen!

I was the kind of man that needed to be moved by God. He did. God moves.

# About The Author

Neil Davies was born in 1975 in South Africa. After graduating high school in 1993, he enlisted in the South African Air Force and eventually joined Air Force Intelligence. Upon successfully completing officer training, he was selected to attend the Military Academy on the west coast of South Africa and graduated at the end of 2001 with a post-graduate degree in computer information systems. After resigning his commission in the Air Force, Neil backpacked in England and Scotland for two years. Upon his return to South Africa, he became the managing editor of a magazine and also wrote scripts for television for a short while. In 2009, he immigrated to the United States and currently lives in North Dakota.

# Part 2

# CONTENTS

# On The Incarnation Of The Word

By St. Athanasius

Athanasius of Alexandria (born circa 296-298-died 2 May 373), also referred to as St. Athanasius the Great, St. Athanasius I of Alexandria, St Athanasius the Confessor and St. Athanasius the Apostolic, was the 20th bishop of Alexandria. His episcopate lasted 45 years, of which over 17 were spent in five exiles ordered by four different Roman emperors. He is considered to be a renowned Christian theologian, a Church Father, the chief defender of Trinitarianism against Arianism, and a noted Egyptian leader of the fourth century. Athanasius is counted as one of the four Great Doctors of the Church in the Roman Catholic Church as well as one of the Great Doctors of the Church in Eastern Orthodoxy, where he is also labelled the "Father of Orthodoxy". He is also celebrated by many Protestants, who label him "Father of The Canon". Athanasius is venerated as a Christian saint, whose feast day is 2 May in Western Christianity, 15 May in the Coptic Orthodox Church, and 18 January in the other Eastern Orthodox Churches. He is venerated by the Roman Catholic Church, Oriental and Eastern Orthodox churches, the Lutherans, and the Anglican Communion.

This translation was made by Sister Penelope Lawson, of the Anglican Community of St. Mary the Virgin in Wantage, England. It was originally published with a byline that reads only "Translated and edited by A Religious of C.S.M.V."

# 1

# CREATION AND THE FALL

(1) In our former book[1] we dealt fully enough with a few of the chief points about the heathen worship of idols, and how those false fears originally arose. We also, by God's grace, briefly indicated that the Word of the Father is Himself divine, that all things that are owe their being to His will and power, and that it is through Him that the Father gives order to creation, by Him that all things are moved, and through Him that they receive their being. Now, Macarius, true lover of Christ, we must take a step further in the faith of our holy religion, and consider also the Word's becoming Man and His divine Appearing in our midst. That mystery the Jews traduce, the Greeks deride, but we adore; and your own love and devotion to the Word also will be the greater, because in His Manhood He seems so little worth. For it is a fact that the more unbelievers pour scorn on Him, so much the more does He make His Godhead evident. The things which they, as men, rule out as impossible, He plainly shows to be possible; that which they deride as unfitting, His goodness makes most fit; and things which these wiseacres laugh at as "human" He by His inherent might declares divine. Thus by what seems His utter poverty and weakness on the cross He overturns the pomp and parade of idols, and quietly and hiddenly wins over the mockers and unbelievers to recognize Him as God.

Now in dealing with these matters it is necessary first to recall what has already been said. You must understand why it is that the Word of

---

1 i.e. the Contra Gentes.

the Father, so great and so high, has been made manifest in bodily form. He has not assumed a body as proper to His own nature, far from it, for as the Word He is without body. He has been manifested in a human body for this reason only, out of the love and goodness of His Father, for the salvation of us men. We will begin, then, with the creation of the world and with God its Maker, for the first fact that you must grasp is this: the renewal of creation has been wrought by the Self-same Word Who made it in the beginning. There is thus no inconsistency between creation and salvation for the One Father has employed the same Agent for both works, effecting the salvation of the world through the same Word Who made it in the beginning.

(2) In regard to the making of the universe and the creation of all things there have been various opinions, and each person has propounded the theory that suited his own taste. For instance, some say that all things are self-originated and, so to speak, haphazard. The Epicureans are among these; they deny that there is any Mind behind the universe at all. This view is contrary to all the facts of experience, their own existence included. For if all things had come into being in this automatic fashion, instead of being the outcome of Mind, though they existed, they would all be uniform and without distinction. In the universe everything would be sun or moon or whatever it was, and in the human body the whole would be hand or eye or foot. But in point of fact the sun and the moon and the earth are all different things, and even within the human body there are different members, such as foot and hand and head. This distinctness of things argues not a spontaneous generation but a prevenient Cause; and from that Cause we can apprehend God, the Designer and Maker of all.

Others take the view expressed by Plato, that giant among the Greeks. He said that God had made all things out of pre-existent and uncreated matter, just as the carpenter makes things only out of wood that already exists. But those who hold this view do not realize that to deny that God is Himself the Cause of matter is to impute limitation to Him, just as it is undoubtedly a limitation on the part of the carpenter that he can make nothing unless he has the wood. How could God be called Maker and Artificer if His ability to make depended on some other cause, namely on matter itself? If He only worked up existing matter and did not

Himself bring matter into being, He would be not the Creator but only a craftsman.

Then, again, there is the theory of the Gnostics, who have invented for themselves an Artificer of all things other than the Father of our Lord Jesus Christ. These simply shut their eyes to the obvious meaning of Scripture. For instance, the Lord, having reminded the Jews of the statement in Genesis, "He Who created them in the beginning made them male and female . . .," and having shown that for that reason a man should leave his parents and cleave to his wife, goes on to say with reference to the Creator, "What therefore God has joined together, let no man put asunder."[1] How can they get a creation independent of the Father out of that? And, again, St. John, speaking all inclusively, says, "All things became by Him and without Him came nothing into being."[2] How then could the Artificer be someone different, other than the Father of Christ?

(3) Such are the notions which men put forward. But the impiety of their foolish talk is plainly declared by the divine teaching of the Christian faith. From it we know that, because there is Mind behind the universe, it did not originate itself; because God is infinite, not finite, it was not made from pre-existent matter, but out of nothing and out of non-existence absolute and utter God brought it into being through the Word. He says as much in Genesis: "In the beginning God created the heavens and the earth;"[3] and again through that most helpful book The Shepherd, "Believe thou first and foremost that there is One God Who created and arranged all things and brought them out of non-existence into being."[4] Paul also indicates the same thing when he says, "By faith we understand that the worlds were framed by the Word of God, so that the things which we see now did not come into being out of things which had previously appeared."[5] For God is good—or rather, of all goodness

1 Matthew 19:4-6

2 John 1:3

3 Genesis 1:1

4 The Shepherd of Hermas, Book II. I

5 Hebrews 11:3

He is Fountainhead, and it is impossible for one who is good to be mean or grudging about anything. Grudging existence to none therefore, He made all things out of nothing through His own Word, our Lord Jesus Christ and of all these His earthly creatures He reserved especial mercy for the race of men. Upon them, therefore, upon men who, as animals, were essentially impermanent, He bestowed a grace which other creatures lacked—namely the impress of His own Image, a share in the reasonable being of the very Word Himself, so that, reflecting Him and themselves becoming reasonable and expressing the Mind of God even as He does, though in limited degree they might continue for ever in the blessed and only true life of the saints in paradise. But since the will of man could turn either way, God secured this grace that He had given by making it conditional from the first upon two things—namely, a law and a place. He set them in His own paradise, and laid upon them a single prohibition. If they guarded the grace and retained the loveliness of their original innocence, then the life of paradise should be theirs, without sorrow, pain or care, and after it the assurance of immortality in heaven. But if they went astray and became vile, throwing away their birth right of beauty, then they would come under the natural law of death and live no longer in paradise, but, dying outside of it, continue in death and in corruption. This is what Holy Scripture tells us, proclaiming the command of God, "Of every tree that is in the garden thou shalt surely eat, but of the tree of the knowledge of good and evil ye shall not eat, but in the day that ye do eat, ye shall surely die."[1] "Ye shall surely die"—not just die only, but remain in the state of death and of corruption.

(4) You may be wondering why we are discussing the origin of men when we set out to talk about the Word's becoming Man. The former subject is relevant to the latter for this reason: it was our sorry case that caused the Word to come down, our transgression that called out His love for us, so that He made haste to help us and to appear among us. It is we who were the cause of His taking human form, and for our salvation that in His great love He was both born and manifested in a human body. For God had made man thus (that is, as an embodied spirit), and had willed that he should remain in incorruption. But

[1] Genesis 2:16

men, having turned from the contemplation of God to evil of their own devising, had come inevitably under the law of death. Instead of remaining in the state in which God had created them, they were in process of becoming corrupted entirely, and death had them completely under its dominion. For the transgression of the commandment was making them turn back again according to their nature; and as they had at the beginning come into being out of non-existence, so were they now on the way to returning, through corruption, to non-existence again. The presence and love of the Word had called them into being; inevitably, therefore when they lost the knowledge of God, they lost existence with it; for it is God alone Who exists, evil is non-being, the negation and antithesis of good. By nature, of course, man is mortal, since he was made from nothing; but he bears also the Likeness of Him Who is, and if he preserves that Likeness through constant contemplation, then his nature is deprived of its power and he remains incorrupt. So is it affirmed in Wisdom: "The keeping of His laws is the assurance of incorruption."[1] And being incorrupt, he would be henceforth as God, as Holy Scripture says, "I have said, Ye are gods and sons of the Highest all of you: but ye die as men and fall as one of the princes."[2]

(5) This, then, was the plight of men. God had not only made them out of nothing, but had also graciously bestowed on them His own life by the grace of the Word. Then, turning from eternal things to things corruptible, by counsel of the devil, they had become the cause of their own corruption in death; for, as I said before, though they were by nature subject to corruption, the grace of their union with the Word made them capable of escaping from the natural law, provided that they retained the beauty of innocence with which they were created. That is to say, the presence of the Word with them shielded them even from natural corruption, as also Wisdom says: "God created man for incorruption and as an image of His own eternity; but by envy of the devil death entered into the world."[3] When this happened, men began to die, and corruption ran riot among them and held sway over them to an

1 Wisdom of Solomon 6:18

2 Psalm 82:6

3 Wisdom of Solomon 2:23

even more than natural degree, because it was the penalty of which God had forewarned them for transgressing the commandment. Indeed, they had in their sinning surpassed all limits; for, having invented wickedness in the beginning and so involved themselves in death and corruption, they had gone on gradually from bad to worse, not stopping at any one kind of evil, but continually, as with insatiable appetite, devising new kinds of sins. Adulteries and thefts were everywhere, murder and rapine filled the earth, law was disregarded in corruption and injustice, all kinds of iniquities were perpetrated by all, both singly and in common. Cities were warring with cities, nations were rising against nations, and the whole earth was rent with factions and battles, while each strove to outdo the other in wickedness. Even crimes contrary to nature were not unknown, but as the martyr-apostle of Christ says: "Their women changed the natural use into that which is against nature; and the men also, leaving the natural use of the woman, flamed out in lust towards each other, perpetrating shameless acts with their own sex, and receiving in their own persons the due recompense of their pervertedness."[1]

---

1 Romans 1:26

# 2

# The Divine Dilemma and its Solution in the Incarnation

(6) We saw in the last chapter that, because death and corruption were gaining ever firmer hold on them, the human race was in process of destruction. Man, who was created in God's image and in his possession of reason reflected the very Word Himself, was disappearing, and the work of God was being undone. The law of death, which followed from the Transgression, prevailed upon us, and from it there was no escape. The thing that was happening was in truth both monstrous and unfitting. It would, of course, have been unthinkable that God should go back upon His word and that man, having transgressed, should not die; but it was equally monstrous that beings which once had shared the nature of the Word should perish and turn back again into non-existence through corruption. It was unworthy of the goodness of God that creatures made by Him should be brought to nothing through the deceit wrought upon man by the devil; and it was supremely unfitting that the work of God in mankind should disappear, either through their own negligence or through the deceit of evil spirits. As, then, the creatures whom He had created reasonable, like the Word, were in fact perishing, and such noble works were on the road to ruin, what then was God, being Good, to do? Was He to let corruption and death have their way with them? In that case, what was the use of having made them in the beginning? Surely it would have been better never to have been created at all than, having been created, to be neglected and perish; and, besides that, such indifference to the ruin of His own work before His very eyes would argue not goodness in God but limitation, and that far more than if He had never created men at all. It was impossible, therefore, that God

should leave man to be carried off by corruption, because it would be unfitting and unworthy of Himself.

(7) Yet, true though this is, it is not the whole matter. As we have already noted, it was unthinkable that God, the Father of Truth, should go back upon His word regarding death in order to ensure our continued existence. He could not falsify Himself; what, then, was God to do? Was He to demand repentance from men for their transgression? You might say that that was worthy of God, and argue further that, as through the Transgression they became subject to corruption, so through repentance they might return to incorruption again. But repentance would not guard the Divine consistency, for, if death did not hold dominion over men, God would still remain untrue. Nor does repentance recall men from what is according to their nature; all that it does is to make them cease from sinning. Had it been a case of a trespass only, and not of a subsequent corruption, repentance would have been well enough; but when once transgression had begun men came under the power of the corruption proper to their nature and were bereft of the grace which belonged to them as creatures in the Image of God. No, repentance could not meet the case. What—or rather Who was it that was needed for such grace and such recall as we required? Who, save the Word of God Himself, Who also in the beginning had made all things out of nothing? His part it was, and His alone, both to bring again the corruptible to incorruption and to maintain for the Father His consistency of character with all. For He alone, being Word of the Father and above all, was in consequence both able to recreate all, and worthy to suffer on behalf of all and to be an ambassador for all with the Father.

(8) For this purpose, then, the incorporeal and incorruptible and immaterial Word of God entered our world. In one sense, indeed, He was not far from it before, for no part of creation had ever been without Him Who, while ever abiding in union with the Father, yet fills all things that are. But now He entered the world in a new way, stooping to our level in His love and Self-revealing to us. He saw the reasonable race, the race of men that, like Himself, expressed the Father's Mind, wasting out of existence, and death reigning over all in corruption. He saw that corruption held us all the closer, because it was the penalty for the Transgression; He saw, too, how unthinkable it would be for the law to

be repealed before it was fulfilled. He saw how unseemly it was that the very things of which He Himself was the Artificer should be disappearing. He saw how the surpassing wickedness of men was mounting up against them; He saw also their universal liability to death. All this He saw and, pitying our race, moved with compassion for our limitation, unable to endure that death should have the mastery, rather than that His creatures should perish and the work of His Father for us men come to nought, He took to Himself a body, a human body even as our own. Nor did He will merely to become embodied or merely to appear; had that been so, He could have revealed His divine majesty in some other and better way. No, He took our body, and not only so, but He took it directly from a spotless, stainless virgin, without the agency of human father—a pure body, untainted by intercourse with man. He, the Mighty One, the Artificer of all, Himself prepared this body in the virgin as a temple for Himself, and took it for His very own, as the instrument through which He was known and in which He dwelt. Thus, taking a body like our own, because all our bodies were liable to the corruption of death, He surrendered His body to death instead of all, and offered it to the Father. This He did out of sheer love for us, so that in His death all might die, and the law of death thereby be abolished because, having fulfilled in His body that for which it was appointed, it was thereafter voided of its power for men. This He did that He might turn again to incorruption men who had turned back to corruption, and make them alive through death by the appropriation of His body and by the grace of His resurrection. Thus He would make death to disappear from them as utterly as straw from fire.

(9) The Word perceived that corruption could not be got rid of otherwise than through death; yet He Himself, as the Word, being immortal and the Father's Son, was such as could not die. For this reason, therefore, He assumed a body capable of death, in order that it, through belonging to the Word Who is above all, might become in dying a sufficient exchange for all, and, itself remaining incorruptible through His indwelling, might thereafter put an end to corruption for all others as well, by the grace of the resurrection. It was by surrendering to death the body which He had taken, as an offering and sacrifice free from every stain, that He forthwith abolished death for His human brethren by the offering of the equivalent. For naturally, since the Word of God was above all, when He offered His own temple and bodily instrument as

a substitute for the life of all, He fulfilled in death all that was required. Naturally also, through this union of the immortal Son of God with our human nature, all men were clothed with incorruption in the promise of the resurrection. For the solidarity of mankind is such that, by virtue of the Word's indwelling in a single human body, the corruption which goes with death has lost its power over all. You know how it is when some great king enters a large city and dwells in one of its houses; because of his dwelling in that single house, the whole city is honored, and enemies and robbers cease to molest it. Even so is it with the King of all; He has come into our country and dwelt in one body amidst the many, and in consequence the designs of the enemy against mankind have been foiled and the corruption of death, which formerly held them in its power, has simply ceased to be. For the human race would have perished utterly had not the Lord and Savior of all, the Son of God, come among us to put an end to death.

(10) This great work was, indeed, supremely worthy of the goodness of God. A king who has founded a city, so far from neglecting it when through the carelessness of the inhabitants it is attacked by robbers, avenges it and saves it from destruction, having regard rather to his own honor than to the people's neglect. Much more, then, the Word of the All-good Father was not unmindful of the human race that He had called to be; but rather, by the offering of His own body He abolished the death which they had incurred, and corrected their neglect by His own teaching. Thus by His own power He restored the whole nature of man. The Savior's own inspired disciples assure us of this. We read in one place: "For the love of Christ constraineth us, because we thus judge that, if One died on behalf of all, then all died, and He died for all that we should no longer live unto ourselves, but unto Him who died and rose again from the dead, even our Lord Jesus Christ."[1] And again another says: "But we behold Him Who hath been made a little lower than the angels, even Jesus, because of the suffering of death crowned with glory and honor, that by the grace of God He should taste of death on behalf of every man." The same writer goes on to point out why it was necessary for God the Word and none other to become Man: "For it became Him, for

---

[1] 2 Corinthians 5:14

Whom are all things and through Whom are all things, in bringing many sons unto glory, to make the Author of their salvation perfect through suffering."[1] He means that the rescue of mankind from corruption was the proper part only of Him Who made them in the beginning. He points out also that the Word assumed a human body, expressly in order that He might offer it in sacrifice for other like bodies: "Since then the children are sharers in flesh and blood, He also Himself assumed the same, in order that through death He might bring to nought Him that hath the power of death, that is to say, the Devil, and might rescue those who all their lives were enslaved by the fear of death."[2] For by the sacrifice of His own body He did two things: He put an end to the law of death which barred our way; and He made a new beginning of life for us, by giving us the hope of resurrection. By man death has gained its power over men; by the Word made Man death has been destroyed and life raised up anew. That is what Paul says, that true servant of Christ: "For since by man came death, by man came also the resurrection of the dead. Just as in Adam all die, even so in Christ shall all be made alive,"[3] and so forth. Now, therefore, when we die we no longer do so as men condemned to death, but as those who are even now in process of rising we await the general resurrection of all, "which in its own times He shall show,"[4] even God Who wrought it and bestowed it on us.

This, then, is the first cause of the Savior's becoming Man. There are, however, other things which show how wholly fitting is His blessed presence in our midst; and these we must now go on to consider.

---

1 Hebrews 2:9

2 Hebrews 2:14

3 1 Corinthians 15:21

4 1 Timothy 6:15

# 3

# The Divine Dilemma and its Solution in the Incarnation—Continued

(11) When God the Almighty was making mankind through His own Word, He perceived that they, owing to the limitation of their nature, could not of themselves have any knowledge of their Artificer, the Incorporeal and Uncreated. He took pity on them, therefore, and did not leave them destitute of the knowledge of Himself, lest their very existence should prove purposeless. For of what use is existence to the creature if it cannot know its Maker? How could men be reasonable beings if they had no knowledge of the Word and Reason of the Father, through Whom they had received their being? They would be no better than the beasts, had they no knowledge save of earthly things; and why should God have made them at all, if He had not intended them to know Him? But, in fact, the good God has given them a share in His own Image, that is, in our Lord Jesus Christ, and has made even themselves after the same Image and Likeness. Why? Simply in order that through this gift of Godlikeness in themselves they may be able to perceive the Image Absolute, that is the Word Himself, and through Him to apprehend the Father; which knowledge of their Maker is for men the only really happy and blessed life.

But, as we have already seen, men, foolish as they are, thought little of the grace they had received, and turned away from God. They defiled their own soul so completely that they not only lost their apprehension of God, but invented for themselves other gods of various kinds. They fashioned idols for themselves in place of the truth and reverenced things that are not, rather than God Who is, as St. Paul says, "worshipping the creature rather than the Creator."[1] Moreover, and much worse, they transferred the honor which is due to God to material objects such as wood and stone, and also to man; and further even than that they went, as we said in our former book. Indeed, so impious were they that they worshipped evil spirits as gods in satisfaction of their lusts. They sacrificed brute beasts and immolated men, as the just due of these deities, thereby bringing themselves more and more under their insane control. Magic arts also were taught among them, oracles in sundry places led men astray, and the cause of everything in human life was traced to the stars as though nothing existed but that which could be seen. In a word, impiety and lawlessness were everywhere, and neither God nor His Word was known. Yet He had not hidden Himself from the sight of men nor given the knowledge of Himself in one way only; but rather He had unfolded it in many forms and by many ways.

(12) God knew the limitation of mankind, you see; and though the grace of being made in His Image was sufficient to give them knowledge of the Word and through Him of the Father, as a safeguard against their neglect of this grace, He provided the works of creation also as means by which the Maker might be known. Nor was this all. Man's neglect of the indwelling grace tends ever to increase; and against this further frailty also God made provision by giving them a law, and by sending prophets, men whom they knew. Thus, if they were tardy in looking up to heaven, they might still gain knowledge of their Maker from those close at hand; for men can learn directly about higher things from other men. Three ways thus lay open to them, by which they might obtain the knowledge of God. They could look up into the immensity of heaven, and by pondering the harmony of creation come to know its Ruler, the Word of the Father, Whose all-ruling providence makes known the Father to all. Or, if this was beyond them, they could converse with holy men, and through them learn to know God, the Artificer of all things, the Father of Christ, and to recognize the worship of idols as the negation of the truth and full of all impiety. Or else, in the third place, they could cease from

---

[1] Romans 1:25

lukewarmness and lead a good life merely by knowing the law. For the law was not given only for the Jews, nor was it solely for their sake that God sent the prophets, though it was to the Jews that they were sent and by the Jews that they were persecuted. The law and the prophets were a sacred school of the knowledge of God and the conduct of the spiritual life for the whole world. So great, indeed, were the goodness and the love of God. Yet men, bowed down by the pleasures of the moment and by the frauds and illusions of the evil spirits, did not lift up their heads towards the truth. So burdened were they with their wickednesses that they seemed rather to be brute beasts than reasonable men, reflecting the very Likeness of the Word.

(13) What was God to do in face of this dehumanising of mankind, this universal hiding of the knowledge of Himself by the wiles of evil spirits? Was He to keep silence before so great a wrong and let men go on being thus deceived and kept in ignorance of Himself? If so, what was the use of having made them in His own Image originally? It would surely have been better for them always to have been brutes, rather than to revert to that condition when once they had shared the nature of the Word. Again, things being as they were, what was the use of their ever having had the knowledge of God? Surely it would have been better for God never to have bestowed it, than that men should subsequently be found unworthy to receive it. Similarly, what possible profit could it be to God Himself, Who made men, if when made they did not worship Him, but regarded others as their makers? This would be tantamount to His having made them for others and not for Himself. Even an earthly king, though he is only a man, does not allow lands that he has colonized to pass into other hands or to desert to other rulers, but sends letters and friends and even visits them himself to recall them to their allegiance, rather than allow His work to be undone. How much more, then, will God be patient and painstaking with His creatures, that they be not led astray from Him to the service of those that are not, and that all the more because such error means for them sheer ruin, and because it is not right that those who had once shared His Image should be destroyed.

What, then, was God to do? What else could He possibly do, being God, but renew His Image in mankind, so that through it men might once more come to know Him? And how could this be done save by the coming of the very Image Himself, our Savior Jesus Christ? Men could not have done it, for they are only made after the Image; nor could angels have done it, for they are not the images of God. The Word of God came in His own Person, because it was He alone, the Image of the Father Who could recreate man made after the Image.

In order to effect this re-creation, however, He had first to do away with death and corruption. Therefore He assumed a human body, in order that in it death might once for all be destroyed, and that men might be renewed according to the Image. The Image of the Father only was sufficient for this need. Here is an illustration to prove it.

(14) You know what happens when a portrait that has been painted on a panel becomes obliterated through external stains. The artist does not throw away the panel, but the subject of the portrait has to come and sit for it again, and then the likeness is re-drawn on the same material. Even so was it with the All-holy Son of God. He, the Image of the Father, came and dwelt in our midst, in order that He might renew mankind made after Himself, and seek out His lost sheep, even as He says in the Gospel: "I came to seek and to save that which was lost."[1] This also explains His saying to the Jews: "Except a man be born anew . . ."[2] a He was not referring to a man's natural birth from his mother, as they thought, but to the re-birth and re-creation of the soul in the Image of God.

Nor was this the only thing which only the Word could do. When the madness of idolatry and irreligion filled the world and the knowledge of God was hidden, whose part was it to teach the world about the Father? Man's, would you say? But men cannot run everywhere over the world, nor would their words carry sufficient weight if they did, nor would they be, unaided, a match for the evil spirits. Moreover, since even the best of men were confused and blinded by evil, how could they convert the souls and minds of others? You cannot put straight in others what is warped in yourself. Perhaps you will say, then, that creation was

---

1 Luke 19:10

2 John 1:3

enough to teach men about the Father. But if that had been so, such great evils would never have occurred. Creation was there all the time, but it did not prevent men from wallowing in error. Once more, then, it was the Word of God, Who sees all that is in man and moves all things in creation, Who alone could meet the needs of the situation. It was His part and His alone, whose ordering of the universe reveals the Father, to renew the same teaching. But how was He to do it? By the same means as before, perhaps you will say, that is, through the works of creation. But this was proven insufficient. Men had neglected to consider the heavens before, and now they were looking in the opposite direction. Wherefore, in all naturalness and fitness, desiring to do good to men, as Man He dwells, taking to Himself a body like the rest; and through His actions done in that body, as it were on their own level, He teaches those who would not learn by other means to know Himself, the Word of God, and through Him the Father.

(15) He deals with them as a good teacher with his pupils, coming down to their level and using simple means. St. Paul says as much: "Because in the wisdom of God the world in its wisdom knew not God, God thought fit through the simplicity of the News proclaimed to save those who believe."[1] Men had turned from the contemplation of God above, and were looking for Him in the opposite direction, down among created things and things of sense. The Savior of us all, the Word of God, in His great love took to Himself a body and moved as Man among men, meeting their senses, so to speak, half way. He became Himself an object for the senses, so that those who were seeking God in sensible things might apprehend the Father through the works which He, the Word of God, did in the body. Human and human minded as men were, therefore, to whichever side they looked in the sensible world they found themselves taught the truth. Were they awe-stricken by creation? They beheld it confessing Christ as Lord. Did their minds tend to regard men as Gods? The uniqueness of the Savior's works marked Him, alone of men, as Son of God. Were they drawn to evil spirits? They saw them driven out by the Lord and learned that the Word of God alone was God and that the evil spirits were not gods at all. Were they

---

1 1 Corinthians 1: 21

inclined to hero-worship and the cult of the dead? Then the fact that the Savior had risen from the dead showed them how false these other deities were, and that the Word of the Father is the one true Lord, the Lord even of death. For this reason was He both born and manifested as Man, for this He died and rose, in order that, eclipsing by His works all other human deeds, He might recall men from all the paths of error to know the Father. As He says Himself, "I came to seek and to save that which was lost."[1]

(16) When, then, the minds of men had fallen finally to the level of sensible things, the Word submitted to appear in a body, in order that He, as Man, might center their senses on Himself, and convince them through His human acts that He Himself is not man only but also God, the Word and Wisdom of the true God. This is what Paul wants to tell us when he says: "That ye, being rooted and grounded in love, may be strong to apprehend with all the saints what is the length and breadth and height and depth, and to know the love of God that surpasses knowledge, so that ye may be filled unto all the fullness of God."[2] The Self-revealing of the Word is in every dimension—above, in creation; below, in the Incarnation; in the depth, in Hades; in the breadth, throughout the world. All things have been filled with the knowledge of God.

For this reason He did not offer the sacrifice on behalf of all immediately He came, for if He had surrendered His body to death and then raised it again at once He would have ceased to be an object of our senses. Instead of that, He stayed in His body and let Himself be seen in it, doing acts and giving signs which showed Him to be not only man, but also God the Word. There were thus two things which the Savior did for us by becoming Man. He banished death from us and made us anew; and, invisible and imperceptible as in Himself He is, He became visible through His works and revealed Himself as the Word of the Father, the Ruler and King of the whole creation.

---

1 Luke 19:10

2 Ephesians 3:17

(17) There is a paradox in this last statement which we must now examine. The Word was not hedged in by His body, nor did His presence in the body prevent His being present elsewhere as well. When He moved His body He did not cease also to direct the universe by His Mind and might. No. The marvellous truth is, that being the Word, so far from being Himself contained by anything, He actually contained all things Himself. In creation He is present everywhere, yet is distinct in being from it; ordering, directing, giving life to all, containing all, yet is He Himself the Uncontained, existing solely in His Father. As with the whole, so also is it with the part. Existing in a human body, to which He Himself gives life, He is still Source of life to all the universe, present in every part of it, yet outside the whole; and He is revealed both through the works of His body and through His activity in the world. It is, indeed, the function of soul to behold things that are outside the body, but it cannot energize or move them. A man cannot transport things from one place to another, for instance, merely by thinking about them; nor can you or I move the sun and the stars just by sitting at home and looking at them. With the Word of God in His human nature, however, it was otherwise. His body was for Him not a limitation, but an instrument, so that He was both in it and in all things, and outside all things, resting in the Father alone. At one and the same time—this is the wonder—as Man He was living a human life, and as Word He was sustaining the life of the universe, and as Son He was in constant union with the Father. Not even His birth from a virgin, therefore, changed Him in any way, nor was He defiled by being in the body. Rather, He sanctified the body by being in it. For His being in everything does not mean that He shares the nature of everything, only that He gives all things their being and sustains them in it. Just as the sun is not defiled by the contact of its rays with earthly objects, but rather enlightens and purifies them, so He Who made the sun is not defiled by being made known in a body, but rather the body is cleansed and quickened by His indwelling, "Who did no sin, neither was guile found in His mouth."[1]

(18) You must understand, therefore, that when writers on this sacred theme speak of Him as eating and drinking and being born, they

---

[1] 1 Peter 2:22

mean that the body, as a body, was born and sustained with the food proper to its nature; while God the Word, Who was united with it, was at the same time ordering the universe and revealing Himself through His bodily acts as not man only but God. Those acts are rightly said to be His acts, because the body which did them did indeed belong to Him and none other; moreover, it was right that they should be thus attributed to Him as Man, in order to show that His body was a real one and not merely an appearance. From such ordinary acts as being born and taking food, He was recognized as being actually present in the body; but by the extraordinary acts which He did through the body He proved Himself to be the Son of God. That is the meaning of His words to the unbelieving Jews: "If I do not the works of My Father, believe Me not; but if I do, even if ye believe not Me, believe My works, that ye may know that the Father is in Me and I in the Father."[1]

Invisible in Himself, He is known from the works of creation; so also, when His Godhead is veiled in human nature, His bodily acts still declare Him to be not man only, but the Power and Word of God. To speak authoritatively to evil spirits, for instance, and to drive them out, is not human but divine; and who could see-Him curing all the diseases to which mankind is prone, and still deem Him mere man and not also God? He cleansed lepers, He made the lame to walk, He opened the ears of the deaf and the eyes of the blind, there was no sickness or weakness that-He did not drive away. Even the most casual observer can see that these were acts of God. The healing of the man born blind, for instance, who but the Father and Artificer of man, the Controller of his whole being, could thus have restored the faculty denied at birth? He Who did thus must surely be Himself the Lord of birth. This is proved also at the outset of His becoming Man. He formed His own body from the virgin; and that is no small proof of His Godhead, since He Who made that was the Maker of all else. And would not anyone infer from the fact of that body being begotten of a virgin only, without human father, that He Who appeared in it was also the Maker and Lord of all beside?

---

[1] John 10:37-38

Again, consider the miracle at Cana. Would not anyone who saw the substance of water transmuted into wine understand that He Who did it was the Lord and Maker of the water that He changed? It was for the same reason that He walked on the sea as on dry land—to prove to the onlookers that He had mastery over all. And the feeding of the multitude, when He made little into much, so that from five loaves five thousand mouths were filled—did not that prove Him none other than the very Lord Whose Mind is over all?

# 4

# The Death of Christ

(19) All these things the Savior thought fit to do, so that, recognizing His bodily acts as works of God, men who were blind to His presence in creation might regain knowledge of the Father. For, as I said before, who that saw His authority over evil spirits and their response to it could doubt that He was, indeed, the Son, the Wisdom and the Power of God? Even the very creation broke silence at His behest and, marvellous to relate, confessed with one voice before the cross, that monument of victory, that He Who suffered thereon in the body was not man only, but Son of God and Savior of all. The sun veiled his face, the earth quaked, the mountains were rent asunder, all men were stricken with awe. These things showed that Christ on the cross was God, and that all creation was His slave and was bearing witness by its fear to the presence of its Master.

Thus, then, God the Word revealed Himself to men through His works. We must next consider the end of His earthly life and the nature of His bodily death. This is, indeed, the very center of our faith, and everywhere you hear men speak of it; by it, too, no less than by His other acts, Christ is revealed as God and Son of God.

(20) We have dealt as far as circumstances and our own understanding permit with the reason for His bodily manifestation. We have seen that to change the corruptible to incorruption was proper to none other than the Savior Himself, Who in the beginning made all things out of nothing; that only the Image of the Father could re-create the likeness of the Image in men, that none save our Lord Jesus Christ

could give to mortals immortality, and that only the Word Who orders all things and is alone the Father's true and sole-begotten Son could teach men about Him and abolish the worship of idols But beyond all this, there was a debt owing which must needs be paid; for, as I said before, all men were due to die. Here, then, is the second reason why the Word dwelt among us, namely that having proved His Godhead by His works, He might offer the sacrifice on behalf of all, surrendering His own temple to death in place of all, to settle man's account with death and free him from the primal transgression. In the same act also He showed Himself mightier than death, displaying His own body incorruptible as the first-fruits of the resurrection.

You must not be surprised if we repeat ourselves in dealing with this subject. We are speaking of the good pleasure of God and of the things which He in His loving wisdom thought fit to do, and it is better to put the same thing in several ways than to run the risk of leaving something out. The body of the Word, then, being a real human body, in spite of its having been uniquely formed from a virgin, was of itself mortal and, like other bodies, liable to death. But the indwelling of the Word loosed it from this natural liability, so that corruption could not touch it. Thus it happened that two opposite marvels took place at once: the death of all was consummated in the Lord's body; yet, because the Word was in it, death and corruption were in the same act utterly abolished. Death there had to be, and death for all, so that the due of all might be paid. Wherefore, the Word, as I said, being Himself incapable of death, assumed a mortal body, that He might offer it as His own in place of all, and suffering for the sake of all through His union with it, "might bring to nought Him that had the power of death, that is, the devil, and might deliver them who all their lifetime were enslaved by the fear of death."[1]

(21) Have no fears then. Now that the common Savior of all has died on our behalf, we who believe in Christ no longer die, as men died aforetime, in fulfilment of the threat of the law. That condemnation has come to an end; and now that, by the grace of the resurrection, corruption has been banished and done away, we are loosed from our

---

[1] Hebrews 2:14

mortal bodies in God's good time for each, so that we may obtain thereby a better resurrection. Like seeds cast into the earth, we do not perish in our dissolution, but like them shall rise again, death having been brought to nought by the grace of the Savior. That is why blessed Paul, through whom we all have surety of the resurrection, says: "This corruptible must put on incorruption and this mortal must put on immortality; but when this corruptible shall have put on incorruption and this mortal shall have put on immortality, then shall be brought to pass the saying that is written, 'Death is swallowed up in victory. O Death, where is thy sting? O Grave, where is thy victory?'"[1]

"Well then," some people may say, "if the essential thing was that He should surrender His body to death in place of all, why did He not do so as Man privately, without going to the length of public crucifixion? Surely it would have been more suitable for Him to have laid aside His body with honor than to endure so shameful a death." But look at this argument closely, and see how merely human it is, whereas what the Savior did was truly divine and worthy of His Godhead for several reasons. The first is this. The death of men under ordinary circumstances is the result of their natural weakness. They are essentially impermanent, so after a time they fall ill and when worn out they die. But the Lord is not like that. He is not weak, He is the Power of God and Word of God and Very Life Itself. If He had died quietly in His bed like other men it would have looked as if He did so in accordance with His nature, and as though He was indeed no more than other men. But because He was Himself Word and Life and Power His body was made strong, and because the death had to be accomplished, He took the occasion of perfecting His sacrifice not from Himself, but from others. How could He fall sick, Who had healed others? Or how could that body weaken and fail by means of which others are made strong? Here, again, you may say, "Why did He not prevent death, as He did sickness?" Because it was precisely in order to be able to die that He had taken a body, and to prevent the death would have been to impede the resurrection. And as to the unsuitability of sickness for His body, as arguing weakness, you may say, "Did He then not hunger?" Yes, He hungered, because that was the

[1] 1 Corinthians 15:53

property of His body, but He did not die of hunger because He Whose body hungered was the Lord. Similarly, though He died to ransom all, He did not see corruption. His body rose in perfect soundness, for it was the body of none other than the Life Himself.

(22) Someone else might say, perhaps, that it would have been better for the Lord to have avoided the designs of the Jews against Him, and so to have guarded His body from death altogether. But see how unfitting this also would have been for Him. Just as it would not have been fitting for Him to give His body to death by His own hand, being Word and being Life, so also it was not consonant with Himself that He should avoid the death inflicted by others. Rather, He pursued it to the uttermost, and in pursuance of His nature neither laid aside His body of His own accord nor escaped the plotting Jews. And this action showed no limitation or weakness in the Word; for He both waited for death in order to make an end of it, and hastened to accomplish it as an offering on behalf of all. Moreover, as it was the death of all mankind that the Savior came to accomplish, not His own, He did not lay aside His body by an individual act of dying, for to Him, as Life, this simply did not belong; but He accepted death at the hands of men, thereby completely to destroy it in His own body.

There are some further considerations which enable one to understand why the Lord's body had such an end. The supreme object of His coming was to bring about the resurrection of the body. This was to be the monument to His victory over death, the assurance to all that He had Himself conquered corruption and that their own bodies also would eventually be incorrupt; and it was in token of that and as a pledge of the future resurrection that He kept His body incorrupt. But there again, if His body had fallen sick and the Word had left it in that condition, how unfitting it would have been! Should He Who healed the bodies of others neglect to keep His own in health? How would His miracles of healing be believed, if this were so? Surely people would either laugh at Him as unable to dispel disease or else consider Him lacking in proper human feeling because He could do so, but did not.

(23) Then, again, suppose without any illness He had just concealed His body somewhere, and then suddenly reappeared and said that He

had risen from the dead. He would have been regarded merely as a teller of tales, and because there was no witness of His death, nobody would believe His resurrection. Death had to precede resurrection, for there could be no resurrection without it. A secret and unwitnessed death would have left the resurrection without any proof or evidence to support it. Again, why should He die a secret death, when He proclaimed the fact of His rising openly? Why should He drive out evil spirits and heal the man blind from birth and change water into wine, all publicly, in order to convince men that He was the Word, and not also declare publicly that incorruptibility of His mortal body, so that He might Himself be believed to be the Life? And how could His disciples have had boldness in speaking of the resurrection unless they could state it as a fact that He had first died? Or how could their hearers be expected to believe their assertion, unless they themselves also had witnessed His death? For if the Pharisees at the time refused to believe and forced others to deny also, though the things had happened before their very eyes, how many excuses for unbelief would they have contrived, if it had taken place secretly? Or how could the end of death and the victory over it have been declared, had not the Lord thus challenged it before the sight of all, and by the incorruption of His body proved that henceforward it was annulled and void?

(24) There are some other possible objections that must be answered. Some might urge that, even granting the necessity of a public death for subsequent belief in the resurrection, it would surely have been better for Him to have arranged an honorable death for Himself, and so to have avoided the ignominy of the cross. But even this would have given ground for suspicion that His power over death was limited to the particular kind of death which He chose for Himself; and that again would furnish excuse for disbelieving the resurrection. Death came to His body, therefore, not from Himself but from enemy action, in order that the Savior might utterly abolish death in whatever form they offered it to Him. A generous wrestler, virile and strong, does not himself choose his antagonists, lest it should be thought that of some of them he is afraid. Rather, he lets the spectators choose them, and that all the more if these are hostile, so that he may overthrow whomsoever they match against him and thus vindicate his superior strength. Even so was it with Christ. He, the Life of all, our Lord and Savior, did not

arrange the manner of his own death lest He should seem to be afraid of some other kind. No. He accepted and bore upon the cross a death inflicted by others, and those others His special enemies, a death which to them was supremely terrible and by no means to be faced; and He did this in order that, by destroying even this death, He might Himself be believed to be the Life, and the power of death be recognized as finally annulled. A marvellous and mighty paradox has thus occurred, for the death which they thought to inflict on Him as dishonor and disgrace has become the glorious monument to death's defeat. Therefore it is also, that He neither endured the death of John, who was beheaded, nor was He sawn asunder, like Isaiah: even in death He preserved His body whole and undivided, so that there should be no excuse hereafter for those who would divide the Church.

(25) So much for the objections of those outside the Church. But if any honest Christian wants to know why He suffered death on the cross and not in some other way, we answer thus: in no other way was it expedient for us, indeed the Lord offered for our sakes the one death that was supremely good. He had come to bear the curse that lay on us; and how could He "become a curse"[1] otherwise than by accepting the accursed death? And that death is the cross, for it is written "Cursed is every one that hangeth on tree."[2] Again, the death of the Lord is the ransom of all, and by it "the middle wall of partition"[3] is broken down and the call of the Gentiles comes about. How could He have called us if He had not been crucified, for it is only on the cross that a man dies with arms outstretched? Here, again, we see the fitness of His death and of those outstretched arms: it was that He might draw His ancient people with the one and the Gentiles with the other, and join both together in Himself. Even so, He foretold the manner of His redeeming death, "I, if I be lifted up, will draw all men unto Myself."[4] Again, the air is the sphere of the devil, the enemy of our race who, having fallen from heaven, endeavors with the other evil spirits who shared in his disobedience both

---

1 Galatians 3:13

2 Galatians 3:13

3 Ephesians 2:14

4 John 7:32

to keep souls from the truth and to hinder the progress of those who are trying to follow it. The apostle refers to this when he says, "According to the prince of the power of the air, of the spirit that now worketh in the sons of disobedience."[1] But the Lord came to overthrow the devil and to purify the air and to make "a way" for us up to heaven, as the apostle says, "through the veil, that is to say, His flesh."[2] This had to be done through death, and by what other kind of death could it be done, save by a death in the air, that is, on the cross? Here, again, you see how right and natural it was that the Lord should suffer thus; for being thus "lifted up," He cleansed the air from all the evil influences of the enemy. "I beheld Satan as lightning falling,"[3] He says; and thus He re-opened the road to heaven, saying again, "Lift up your gates, O ye princes, and be ye lift up, ye everlasting doors."[4] For it was not the Word Himself Who needed an opening of the gates, He being Lord of all, nor was any of His works closed to their Maker. No, it was we who needed it, we whom He Himself upbore in His own body—that body which He first offered to death on behalf of all, and then made through it a path to heaven.

---

1 Ephesians 2:2

2 Hebrews 10:20

3 Luke 10:18

4 Psalm 24:7

# 5

## The Resurrection

(26) Fitting indeed, then, and wholly consonant was the death on the cross for us; and we can see how reasonable it was, and why it is that the salvation of the world could be accomplished in no other way. Even on the cross He did not hide Himself from sight; rather, He made all creation witness to the presence of its Maker. Then, having once let it be seen that it was truly dead, He did not allow that temple of His body to linger long, but forthwith on the third day raised it up, impassable and incorruptible, the pledge and token of His victory.

It was, of course, within His power thus to have raised His body and displayed it as alive directly after death. But the all-wise Savior did not do this, lest some should deny that it had really or completely died. Besides this, had the interval between His death and resurrection been but two days, the glory of His incorruption might not have appeared. He waited one whole day to show that His body was really dead, and then on the third day showed it incorruptible to all. The interval was no longer, lest people should have forgotten about it and grown doubtful whether it were in truth the same body. No, while the affair was still ringing in their ears and their eyes were still straining and their minds in turmoil, and while those who had put Him to death were still on the spot and themselves witnessing to the fact of it, the Son of God after three days showed His once dead body immortal and incorruptible; and it was evident to all that it was from no natural weakness that the body which the Word indwelt had died, but in order that in it by the Savior's power death might be done away.

(27) A very strong proof of this destruction of death and its conquest by the cross is supplied by a present fact, namely this. All the disciples of Christ despise death; they take the offensive against it and, instead of fearing it, by the sign of the cross and by faith in Christ trample on it as on something dead. Before the divine sojourn of the Savior, even the holiest of men were afraid of death, and mourned the dead as those who perish. But now that the Savior has raised His body, death is no longer terrible, but all those who believe in Christ tread it underfoot as nothing, and prefer to die rather than to deny their faith in Christ, knowing full well that when they die they do not perish, but live indeed, and become incorruptible through the resurrection. But that devil who of old wickedly exulted in death, now that the pains of death are loosed, he alone it is who remains truly dead. There is proof of this too; for men who, before they believe in Christ, think death horrible and are afraid of it, once they are converted despise it so completely that they go eagerly to meet it, and themselves become witnesses of the Savior's resurrection from it. Even children hasten thus to die, and not men only, but women train themselves by bodily discipline to meet it. So weak has death become that even women, who used to be taken in by it, mock at it now as a dead thing robbed of all its strength. Death has become like a tyrant who has been completely conquered by the legitimate monarch; bound hand and foot the passers-by sneer at him, hitting him and abusing him, no longer afraid of his cruelty and rage, because of the king who has conquered him. So has death been conquered and branded for what it is by the Savior on the cross. It is bound hand and foot, all who are in Christ trample it as they pass and as witnesses to Him deride it, scoffing and saying, "O Death, where is thy victory? O Grave, where is thy sting?"[1]

(28) Is this a slender proof of the impotence of death, do you think? Or is it a slight indication of the Savior's victory over it, when boys and young girls who are in Christ look beyond this present life and train themselves to die? Every one is by nature afraid of death and of bodily dissolution; the marvel of marvels is that he who is enfolded in the faith of the cross despises this natural fear and for the sake of the cross is no

---

[1] 1 Corinthians 15:55

longer cowardly in face of it. The natural property of fire is to burn. Suppose, then, that there was a substance such as the Indian asbestos is said to be, which had no fear of being burnt, but rather displayed the impotence of the fire by proving itself unburnable. If anyone doubted the truth of this, all he need do would be to wrap himself up in the substance in question and then touch the fire. Or, again, to revert to our former figure, if anyone wanted to see the tyrant bound and helpless, who used to be such a terror to others, he could do so simply by going into the country of the tyrant's conqueror. Even so, if anyone still doubts the conquest of death, after so many proofs and so many martyrdoms in Christ and such daily scorn of death by His truest servants, he certainly does well to marvel at so great a thing, but he must not be obstinate in unbelief and disregard of plain facts. No, he must be like the man who wants to prove the property of the asbestos, and like him who enters the conqueror's dominions to see the tyrant bound. He must embrace the faith of Christ, this disbeliever in the conquest of death, and come to His teaching. Then he will see how impotent death is and how completely conquered. Indeed, there have been many former unbelievers and deriders who, after they became believers, so scorned death as even themselves to become martyrs for Christ's sake.

(29) If, then, it is by the sign of the cross and by faith in Christ that death is trampled underfoot, it is clear that it is Christ Himself and none other Who is the Archvictor over death and has robbed it of its power. Death used to be strong and terrible, but now, since the sojourn of the Savior and the death and resurrection of His body, it is despised; and obviously it is by the very Christ Who mounted on the cross that it has been destroyed and vanquished finally. When the sun rises after the night and the whole world is lit up by it, nobody doubts that it is the sun which has thus shed its light everywhere and driven away the dark. Equally clear is it, since this utter scorning and trampling down of death has ensued upon the Savior's manifestation in the body and His death on the cross, that it is He Himself Who brought death to nought and daily raises monuments to His victory in His own disciples. How can you think otherwise, when you see men naturally weak hastening to death, unafraid at the prospect of corruption, fearless of the descent into Hades, even indeed with eager soul provoking it, not shrinking from tortures, but preferring thus to rush on death for Christ's sake, rather

than to remain in this present life? If you see with your own eyes men and women and children, even, thus welcoming death for the sake of Christ's religion, how can you be so utterly silly and incredulous and maimed in your mind as not to realize that Christ, to Whom these all bear witness, Himself gives the victory to each, making death completely powerless for those who hold His faith and bear the sign of the cross? No one in his senses doubts that a snake is dead when he sees it trampled underfoot, especially when he knows how savage it used to be; nor, if he sees boys making fun of a lion, does he doubt that the brute is either dead or completely bereft of strength. These things can be seen with our own eyes, and it is the same with the conquest of death. Doubt no longer, then, when you see death mocked and scorned by those who believe in Christ, that by Christ death was destroyed, and the corruption that goes with it resolved and brought to end.

(30) What we have said is, indeed, no small proof of the destruction of death and of the fact that the cross of the Lord is the monument to His victory. But the resurrection of the body to immortality, which results henceforward from the work of Christ, the common Savior and true Life of all, is more effectively proved by facts than by words to those whose mental vision is sound. For, if, as we have shown, death was destroyed and everybody tramples on it because of Christ, how much more did He Himself first trample and destroy it in His own body! Death having been slain by Him, then, what other issue could there be than the resurrection of His body and its open demonstration as the monument of His victory? How could the destruction of death have been manifested at all, had not the Lord's body been raised? But if anyone finds even this insufficient, let him find proof of what has been said in present facts. Dead men cannot take effective action; their power of influence on others lasts only till the grave. Deeds and actions that energize others belong only to the living. Well, then, look at the facts in this case. The Savior is working mightily among men, every day He is invisibly persuading numbers of people all over the world, both within and beyond the Greek-speaking world, to accept His faith and be obedient to His teaching. Can anyone, in face of this, still doubt that He has risen and lives, or rather that He is Himself the Life? Does a dead man prick the consciences of men, so that they throw all the traditions of their fathers to the winds and bow down before the teaching of Christ? If He is no longer active in the

world, as He must needs be if He is dead, how is it that He makes the living to cease from their activities, the adulterer from his adultery, the murderer from murdering, the unjust from avarice, while the profane and godless man becomes religious? If He did not rise, but is still dead, how is it that He routs and persecutes and overthrows the false gods, whom unbelievers think to be alive, and the evil spirits whom they worship? For where Christ is named, idolatry is destroyed and the fraud of evil spirits is exposed; indeed, no such spirit can endure that Name, but takes to flight on sound of it. This is the work of One Who lives, not of one dead; and, more than that, it is the work of God. It would be absurd to say that the evil spirits whom He drives out and the idols which He destroys are alive, but that He Who drives out and destroys, and Whom they themselves acknowledge to be Son of God, is dead.

(31) In a word, then, those who disbelieve in the resurrection have no support in facts, if their gods and evil spirits do not drive away the supposedly dead Christ. Rather, it is He Who convicts them of being dead. We are agreed that a dead person can do nothing: yet the Savior works mightily every day, drawing men to religion, persuading them to virtue, teaching them about immortality, quickening their thirst for heavenly things, revealing the knowledge of the Father, inspiring strength in face of death, manifesting Himself to each, and displacing the irreligion of idols; while the gods and evil spirits of the unbelievers can do none of these things, but rather become dead at Christ's presence, all their ostentation barren and void. By the sign of the cross, on the contrary, all magic is stayed, all sorcery confounded, all the idols are abandoned and deserted, and all senseless pleasure ceases, as the eye of faith looks up from earth to heaven. Whom, then, are we to call dead? Shall we call Christ dead, Who effects all this? But the dead have not the faculty to effect anything. Or shall we call death dead, which effects nothing whatever, but lies as lifeless and ineffective as are the evil spirits and the idols? The Son of God, "living and effective,"[1] is active every day and effects the salvation of all; but death is daily proved to be stripped of all its strength, and it is the idols and the evil spirits who are dead, not He. No room for doubt remains, therefore, concerning the resurrection of His body.

---

[1] Hebrews 4:12

Indeed, it would seem that he who disbelieves this bodily rising of the Lord is ignorant of the power of the Word and Wisdom of God. If He took a body to Himself at all, and made it His own in pursuance of His purpose, as we have shown that He did, what was the Lord to do with it, and what was ultimately to become of that body upon which the Word had descended? Mortal and offered to death on behalf of all as it was, it could not but die; indeed, it was for that very purpose that the Savior had prepared it for Himself. But on the other hand it could not remain dead, because it had become the very temple of Life. It therefore died, as mortal, but lived again because of the Life within it; and its resurrection is made known through its works.

(32) It is, indeed, in accordance with the nature of the invisible God that He should be thus known through His works; and those who doubt the Lord's resurrection because they do not now behold Him with their eyes, might as well deny the very laws of nature. They have ground for disbelief when works are lacking; but when the works cry out and prove the fact so clearly, why do they deliberately deny the risen life so manifestly shown? Even if their mental faculties are defective, surely their eyes can give them irrefragable proof of the power and Godhead of Christ. A blind man cannot see the sun, but he knows that it is above the earth from the warmth which it affords; similarly, let those who are still in the blindness of unbelief recognize the Godhead of Christ and the resurrection which He has brought about through His manifested power in others. Obviously He would not be expelling evil spirits and despoiling idols, if He were dead, for the evil spirits would not obey one who was dead. If, on the other hand, the very naming of Him drives them forth, He clearly is not dead; and the more so that the spirits, who perceive things unseen by men, would know if He were so and would refuse to obey Him. But, as a matter of fact, what profane persons doubt, the evil spirits know—namely that He is God; and for that reason they flee from Him and fall at His feet, crying out even as they cried when He was in the body, "We know Thee Who Thou art, the Holy One of God," and, "Ah, what have I in common with Thee, Thou Son of God? I implore Thee, torment me not."[1]

---

[1] Luke 4:34 and Mark 5:7

Both from the confession of the evil spirits and from the daily witness of His works, it is manifest, then, and let none presume to doubt it, that the Savior has raised His own body, and that He is very Son of God, having His being from God as from a Father, Whose Word and Wisdom and Whose Power He is. He it is Who in these latter days assumed a body for the salvation of us all, and taught the world concerning the Father. He it is Who has destroyed death and freely graced us all with incorruption through the promise of the resurrection, having raised His own body as its first—fruits, and displayed it by the sign of the cross as the monument to His victory over death and its corruption.

# 6

# REFUTATION OF THE JEWS

(33) We have dealt thus far with the Incarnation of our Savior, and have found clear proof of the resurrection of His Body and His victory over death. Let us now go further and investigate the unbelief and the ridicule with which Jews and Gentiles respectively regard these same facts. It seems that in both cases the points at issue are the same, namely the unfittingness or incongruity (as it seems to them) alike of the cross and of the Word's becoming man at all. But we have no hesitation in taking up the argument against these objectors, for the proofs on our side are extremely clear.

First, then, we will consider the Jews. Their unbelief has its refutation in the Scriptures which even themselves read; for from cover to cover the inspired Book clearly teaches these things both in its entirety and in its actual words. Prophets foretold the marvel of the Virgin and of the Birth from her, saying, "Behold, a virgin shall conceive and bear a son, and they shall call his name 'Emmanuel,' which means 'God is with us.'"[1] And Moses, that truly great one in whose word the Jews trust so implicitly, he also recognized the importance and truth of the matter. He puts it thus: "There shall arise a star from Jacob and a man from Israel, and he shall break in pieces the rulers of Moab.[2] And, again, "How lovely are thy dwellings, O Jacob, thy tents, O Israel! Like woodland valleys they give shade, and like parks by rivers, like tents which the Lord has

1 Isaiah 7:14

2 Numbers 24:17

pitched, like cedar-trees by streams. There shall come forth a Man from among his seed, and he shall rule over many peoples."[1] And, again, Isaiah says, "Before the Babe shall be old enough to call father or mother, he shall take the power of Damascus and the spoils of Samaria from under the eyes of the king of Assyria."[2] These words, then, foretell that a Man shall appear. And Scripture proclaims further that He that is to come is Lord of all. These are the words, "Behold, the Lord sitteth on an airy cloud and shall come into Egypt, and the man-made images of Egypt shall be shaken."[3] And it is from Egypt also that the Father calls him back, saying, "Out of Egypt have I called My Son."[4]

(34) Moreover, the Scriptures are not silent even about His death. On the contrary, they refer to it with the utmost clearness. They have not feared to speak also of the cause of it. He endures it, they say, not for His own sake, but for the sake of bringing immortality and salvation to all, and they record also the plotting of the Jews against Him and all the indignities which He suffered at their hands. Certainly nobody who reads the Scriptures can plead ignorance of the facts as an excuse for error! There is this passage, for instance: "A man that is afflicted and knows how to bear weakness, for His face is turned away. He was dishonored and not considered, He bears our sins and suffers for our sakes. And we for our part thought Him distressed and afflicted and ill-used; but it was for our sins that He was wounded and for our lawlessness that He was made weak. Chastisement for our peace was upon Him, and by His bruising we are healed."[5] O marvel at the love of the Word for men, for it is on our account that He is dishonored, so that we may be brought to honor. "For all we," it goes on, "have strayed like sheep, man has strayed from his path, and the Lord has given Him up for our sins; and He Himself did not open His mouth at the ill-treatment. Like a sheep He was led to slaughter, and as a lamb is dumb before its shearer, so He opened not His mouth; in His humiliation His judgment was taken

---

1 Numbers 24:5-7

2 Isaiah 8:4

3 Isaiah 19:1

4 Hosea 11:1

5 Isaiah 53:3-5

away."[1] And then Scripture anticipates the surmises of any who might think from His suffering thus that He was just an ordinary man, and shows what power worked in His behalf. "Who shall declare of what lineage He comes?" it says, "for His life is exalted from the earth. By the lawlessnesses of the people was He brought to death, and I will give the wicked in return for His burial and the rich in return for His death. For He did no lawlessness, neither was deceit found in His mouth. And the Lord wills to heal Him of His affliction."[2]

(35) You have heard the prophecy of His death, and now, perhaps, you want to know what indications there are about the cross. Even this is not passed over in silence: on the contrary, the sacred writers proclaim it with the utmost plainness. Moses foretells it first, and that right loudly, when he says, "You shall see your Life hanging before your eyes, and shall not believe."[3] After him the prophets also give their witness, saying, "But I as an innocent lamb brought to be offered was yet ignorant of it. They plotted evil against Me, saying, 'Come, let us cast wood into His bread, and wipe Him out from the land of the living."[4] And, again, "They pierced My hands and My feet, they counted all My bones, they divided My garments for themselves and cast lots for My clothing."[5] Now a death lifted up and that takes place on wood can be none other than the death of the cross; moreover, it is only in that death that the hands and feet are pierced. Besides this, since the Savior dwelt among men, all nations everywhere have begun to know God; and this too Holy Writ expressly mentions. "There shall be the Root of Jesse," it says, "and he who rises up to rule the nations, on Him nations shall set their hope."[6]

These are just a few things in proof of what has taken place; but indeed all Scripture teems with disproof of Jewish unbelief. For example, which of the righteous men and holy prophets and patriarchs of whom

---

1 Isaiah 53:6-8

2 Isaiah 53:8-10

3 Deuteronomy 28:66

4 Jeremiah 11:19

5 Psalm 22:16-18

6 Isaiah 11:10

the Divine Scriptures tell ever had his bodily birth from a virgin only? Was not Abel born of Adam, Enoch of Jared, Noah of Lamech, Abraham of Terah, Isaac of Abraham, and Jacob of Isaac? Was not Judah begotten by Jacob and Moses and Aaron by Ameram? Was not Samuel the son of Elkanah, David of Jesse, Solomon of David, Hezekiah of Ahaz, Josiah of Amon, Isaiah of Amos, Jeremiah of Hilkiah and Ezekiel of Buzi? Had not each of these a father as author of his being? So who is He that is born of a virgin only, that sign of which the prophet makes so much? Again, which of all those people had his birth announced to the world by a star in the heavens? When Moses was born his parents hid him. David was unknown even in his own neighborhood, so that mighty Samuel himself was ignorant of his existence and asked whether Jesse had yet another son. Abraham again became known to his neighbors as a great man only after his birth. But with Christ it was otherwise. The witness to His birth was not man, but a star shining in the heavens whence He was coming down.

(36) Then, again, what king that ever was reigned and took trophies from his enemies before he had strength to call father or mother? Was not David thirty years old when he came to the throne and Solomon a grown young man? Did not Joash enter on his reign at the age of seven, and Josiah, some time after him, at about the same age, both of them fully able by that time to call father or mother? Who is there, then, that was reigning and despoiling his enemies almost before he was born? Let the Jews, who have investigated the matter, tell us if there was ever such a king in Israel or Judah—a king upon whom all the nations set their hopes and had peace, instead of being at enmity with him on every side! As long as Jerusalem stood there was constant war between them, and they all fought against Israel. The Assyrians oppressed Israel, the Egyptians persecuted them, the Babylonians fell upon them, and, strange to relate, even the Syrians their neighbors were at war with them. And did not David fight with Moab and smite the Syrians, and Hezekiah quail at the boasting of Sennacherib? Did not Amalek make war on Moses and the Amorites oppose him, and did not the inhabitants of Jericho array themselves against Joshua the son of Nun? Did not the nations always regard Israel with implacable hostility? Then it is worth inquiring who it is, on whom the nations are to set their hopes. Obviously there must be someone, for the prophet could not have told a lie. But did any of the

holy prophets or of the early patriarchs die on the cross for the salvation of all? Was any of them wounded and killed for the healing of all? Did the idols of Egypt fall down before any righteous man or king that came there? Abraham came there certainly, but idolatry prevailed just the same; and Moses was born there, but the mistaken worship was unchanged.

(37) Again, does Scripture tell of anyone who was pierced in hands and feet or hung upon a tree at all, and by means of a cross perfected his sacrifice for the salvation of all? It was not Abraham, for he died in his bed, as did also Isaac and Jacob. Moses and Aaron died in the mountain, and David ended his days in his house, without anybody having plotted against him. Certainly he had been sought by Saul, but he was preserved unharmed. Again Isaiah was sawn asunder, but he was not hung on a tree. Jeremiah was shamefully used, but he did not die under condemnation. Ezekiel suffered, but he did so, not on behalf of the people, but only to signify to them what was going to happen. Moreover, all these even when they suffered were but men, like other men; but He Whom the Scriptures declare to suffer on behalf of all is called not merely man but Life of all, although in point of fact He did share our human nature. "You shall see your Life hanging before your eyes," they say, and "Who shall declare of what lineage He comes?" With all the saints we can trace their descent from the beginning, and see exactly how each came to be; but the Divine Word maintains that we cannot declare the lineage of Him Who is the Life. Who is it, then, of Whom Holy Writ thus speaks? Who is there so great that even the prophets foretell of Him such mighty things? There is indeed no one in the Scriptures at all, save the common Savior of all, the Word of God, our Lord Jesus Christ. He it is that proceeded from a virgin, and appeared as man on earth, He it is Whose earthly lineage cannot be declared, because He alone derives His body from no human father, but from a virgin alone. We can trace the paternal descent of David and Moses and of all the patriarchs. But with the Savior we cannot do so, for it was He Himself Who caused the star to announce His bodily birth, and it was fitting that the Word, when He came down from heaven, should have His sign in heaven too, and fitting that the King of creation on His coming forth should be visibly recognized by all the world. He was actually born in Judea, yet men from Persia came to worship Him. He it is Who won victory from His demon foes and trophies from the idolaters even before His bodily

appearing—namely, all the heathen who from every region have abjured the tradition of their fathers and the false worship of idols and are now placing their hope in Christ and transferring their allegiance to Him. The thing is happening before our very eyes, here in Egypt; and thereby another prophecy is fulfilled, for at no other time have the Egyptians ceased from their false worship save when the Lord of all, riding as on a cloud, came down here in the body and brought the error of idols to nothing and won over everybody to Himself and through Himself to the Father. He it is Who was crucified with the sun and moon as witnesses; and by His death salvation has come to all men, and all creation has been redeemed. He is the Life of all, and He it is Who like a sheep gave up His own body to death, His life for ours and our salvation.

(38) Yet the Jews disbelieve this. This argument does not satisfy them. Well, then, let them be persuaded by other things in their own oracles. Of whom, for instance, do the prophets say "I was made manifest to those who did not seek Me, I was found by those who had not asked for Me? I said, 'See, here am I,' to the nation that had not called upon My Name. I stretched out My hands to a disobedient and gainsaying people."[1] Who is this person that was made manifest, one might ask the Jews? If the prophet is speaking of himself, then they must tell us how he was first hidden, in order to be manifested afterwards. And, again, what kind of man is this prophet, who was not only revealed after being hidden, but also stretched out his hands upon the cross? Those things happened to none of those righteous men: they happened only to the Word of God Who, being by nature without body, on our account appeared in a body and suffered for us all. And if even this is not enough for them, there is other overwhelming evidence by which they may be silenced. The Scripture says, "Be strong, hands that hang down and feeble knees, take courage, you of little faith, be strong and do not fear. See, our God will recompense judgment, He Himself will come and save us. Then the eyes of blind men shall be opened and the ears of deaf men shall hear, and stammerers shall speak distinctly."[2] What can they say to this, or how can they look it in the face at all? For the prophecy

---

1 Isaiah 65:1-2

2 Isaiah 35:3-6

does not only declare that God will dwell here, it also makes known the signs and the time of His coming. When God comes, it says, the blind will see, the lame will walk, the deaf will hear and the stammerers will speak distinctly. Can the Jews tell us when such signs occurred in Israel, or when anything of the kind took place at all in Jewry? The leper Naaman was cleansed, it is true, but no deaf man heard nor did any lame man walk. Elijah raised a dead person and so did Elisha; but no one blind from birth received his sight. To raise a dead person is a great thing indeed, but it is not such as the Savior did. And surely, since the Scriptures have not kept silence about the leper and the dead son of the widow, if a lame man had walked and a blind man had received his sight, they would have mentioned these as well. Their silence on these points proves that the events never took place. When therefore did these things happen, unless when the Word of God Himself came in the body? Was it not when He came that lame men walked and stammerers spoke clearly and men blind from birth were given sight? And the Jews who saw it themselves testified to the fact that such things had never before occurred. "Since the world began," they said, "it has never been heard of that anyone should open the eyes of a man born blind. If this Man were not from God, He could do nothing."[1]

(39) But surely they cannot fight against plain facts. So it may be that, without denying what is written, they will maintain that they are still waiting for these things to happen, and that the Word of God is yet to come, for that is a theme on which they are always harping most brazenly, in spite of all the evidence against them. But they shall be refuted on this supreme point more clearly than on any, and that not by ourselves but by the most wise Daniel, for he signifies the actual date of the Savior's coming as well as His Divine sojourn in our midst. "Seventy weeks," he says, "are cut short upon thy people and upon the holy city, to make a complete end of sin and for sins to be sealed up and iniquities blotted out, and to make reconciliation for iniquity and to seal vision and prophet, and to anoint a Holy One of holies. And thou shalt know and understand from the going forth of the Word to answer,[2]

1 John 9:32-33

2 "Answer" is LXX misreading for Hebrew "restore."

and to build Jerusalem, until Christ the Prince."[1] In regard to the other prophecies, they may possibly be able to find excuses for deferring their reference to a future time, but what can they say to this one? How can they face it at all? Not only does it expressly mention the Anointed One, that is the Christ, it even declares that He Who is to be anointed is not man only, but the Holy One of holies! And it says that Jerusalem is to stand till His coming, and that after it prophet and vision shall cease in Israel! David was anointed of old, and Solomon, and Hezekiah; but then Jerusalem and the place stood, and prophets were prophesying, Gad and Asaph and Nathan, and later Isaiah and Hosea and Amos and others. Moreover, those men who were anointed were called holy certainly, but none of them was called the Holy of holies. Nor is it any use for the Jews to take refuge in the Captivity, and say that Jerusalem did not exist then, for what about the prophets? It is a fact that at the outset of the Exile Daniel and Jeremiah were there, and Ezekiel and Haggai and Zechariah also prophesied.

(40) So the Jews are indulging in fiction, and transferring present time to future. When did prophet and vision cease from Israel? Was it not when Christ came, the Holy One of holies? It is, in fact, a sign and notable proof of the coming of the Word that Jerusalem no longer stands, neither is prophet raised up nor vision revealed among them. And it is natural that it should be so, for when He that was signified had come, what need was there any longer of any to signify Him? And when the Truth had come, what further need was there of the shadow? On His account only they prophesied continually, until such time as Essential Righteousness has come, Who was made the Ransom for the sins of all. For the same reason Jerusalem stood until the same time, in order that there men might premeditate the types before the Truth was known. So, of course, once the Holy One of holies had come, both vision and prophecy were sealed. And the kingdom of Jerusalem ceased at the same time, because kings were to be anointed among them only until the Holy of holies had been anointed. Moses also prophesies that the kingdom of the Jews shall stand until His time, saying, "A ruler shall not fail from Judah nor a prince from his loins, until the things laid up

---

[1] Daniel 9:24-25

for him shall come and the Expectation of the nations Himself."[1] And that is why the Savior Himself was always proclaiming "The law and the prophets prophesied until John."[2] So if there is still king or prophet or vision among the Jews, they do well to deny that Christ is come; but if there is neither king nor vision, and since that time all prophecy has been sealed and city and temple taken, how can they be so irreligious, how can they so flaunt the facts, as to deny Christ Who has brought it all about? Again, they see the heathen forsaking idols and setting their hopes through Christ on the God of Israel; why do they yet deny Christ Who after the flesh was born of the root of Jesse and reigns henceforward? Of course, if the heathen were worshipping some other god, and not confessing the God of Abraham and Isaac and Jacob and Moses, then they would do well to argue that God had not come. But if the heathen are honoring the same God Who gave the law to Moses and the promises to Abraham—the God Whose word too the Jews dishonored, why do they not recognize or rather why do they deliberately refuse to see that the Lord of Whom the Scriptures prophesied has shone forth to the world and appeared to it in a bodily form? Scripture declares it repeatedly. "The Lord God has appeared to us,"[3] and again, "He sent forth His Word and healed them."[4] And again, "It was no ambassador, no angel who saved us, but the Lord Himself."[5] The Jews are afflicted like some demented person who sees the earth lit up by the sun, but denies the sun that lights it up! What more is there for their Expected One to do when he comes? To call the heathen? But they are called already. To put an end to prophet and king and vision? But this too has already happened. To expose the Goddenyingness of idols? It is already exposed and condemned. Or to destroy death? It is already destroyed. What then has not come to pass that the Christ must do? What is there left out or unfulfilled that the Jews should disbelieve so light-heartedly? The plain fact is, as I say, that there is no longer any king or prophet nor Jerusalem nor sacrifice nor vision among them; yet the whole earth is

---

[1] Genesis 49:10

[2] Matthew 11:13

[3] Psalm 118:27

[4] Psalm 57:20

[5] Isaiah 63:9

filled with the knowledge of God, and the Gentiles, forsaking atheism, are now taking refuge with the God of Abraham through the Word, our Lord Jesus Christ.

Surely, then, it must be plain even to the most shameless that the Christ has come, and that He has enlightened all men everywhere, and given them the true and divine teaching about His Father.

Thus the Jews may be refuted by these and other arguments from the Divine teaching.

# 7

## Refutation of the Gentiles

(41) We come now to the unbelief of the Gentiles; and this is indeed a matter for complete astonishment, for they laugh at that which is no fit subject for mockery, yet fail to see the shame and ridiculousness of their own idols. But the arguments on our side do not lack weight, so we will confute them too on reasonable grounds, chiefly from what we ourselves also see.

First of all, what is there in our belief that is unfitting or ridiculous? Is it only that we say that the Word has been manifested in a body? Well, if they themselves really love the truth, they will agree with us that this involved no unfittingness at all. If they deny that there is a Word of God at all, that will be extraordinary, for then they will be ridiculing what they do not know. But suppose they confess that there is a Word of God, that He is the Governor of all things, that in Elim the Father wrought the creation, that by His providence the whole receives light and life and being, and that He is King over all, so that He is known by means of the works of His providence, and through Him the Father. Suppose they confess all this, what then? Are they not unknowingly turning the ridicule against themselves? The Greek philosophers say that the universe is a great body, and they say truly, for we perceive the universe and its parts with our senses. But if the Word of God is in the universe, which is a body, and has entered into it in its every part, what is there surprising or unfitting in our saying that He has entered also into human nature? If it were unfitting for Him to have embodied Himself at all, then it would be unfitting for Him to have entered into the universe, and to be giving light and movement by His providence to all things in it, because the universe, as we have seen, is itself a body. But if it is right and fitting for Him to enter into the universe and to reveal Himself through it, then, because humanity is part of the universe along with the rest, it is no less fitting for Him to appear in a human body, and to enlighten and to work through that. And surely if it were wrong for a part of the universe to have been used to reveal His Divinity to men, it would be much more wrong that He should be so revealed by the whole!

(42) Take a parallel case. A man's personality actuates and quickens his whole body. If anyone said it was unsuitable for the man's power to be in the toe, he would be thought silly, because, while granting that a man penetrates and actuates the whole of his body, he denied his presence in the part. Similarly, no one who admits the presence of the Word of God in the universe as a whole should think it unsuitable for a single human body to be by Him actuated and enlightened.

But is it, perhaps, because humanity is a thing created and brought into being out of non-existence that they regard as unfitting the manifestation of the Savior in our nature? If so, it is high time that they spurned Him from creation too; for it, too, has been brought out of non-being into being by the Word. But if, on the other hand, although creation is a thing that has been made, it is not unsuitable for the Word to be present in it, then neither is it unsuitable for Him to be in man. Man is a part of the creation, as I said before; and the reasoning which applies to one applies to the other. All things derive from the Word their light and movement and life, as the Gentile authors themselves say, "In Him we live and move and have our being."[1] Very well then. That being so, it is by no means unbecoming that the Word should dwell in man. So if, as we say, the Word has used that in which He is as the means of His self-manifestation, what is there ridiculous in that? He could not have used it had He not been present in it; but we have already admitted that He is present both in the whole and in the parts. What, then, is there incredible in His manifesting Himself through that in which He is? By His own power He enters completely into each and all, and orders them throughout ungrudgingly; and, had He so willed, He could have revealed

1 See Acts 17:28

Himself and His Father by means of sun or moon or sky or earth or fire or water. Had He done so, no one could rightly have accused Him of acting unbecomingly, for He sustains in one whole all things at once, being present and invisibly revealed not only in the whole, but also in each particular part. This being so, and since, moreover, He has willed to reveal Himself through men, who are part of the whole, there can be nothing ridiculous in His using a human body to manifest the truth and knowledge of the Father. Does not the mind of man pervade his entire being, and yet find expression through one part only, namely the tongue? Does anybody say on that account that Mind has degraded itself? Of course not. Very well, then, no more is it degrading for the Word, Who pervades all things, to have appeared in a human body. For, as I said before, if it were unfitting for Him thus to indwell the part, it would be equally so for Him to exist within the whole.

(43) Some may then ask, why did He not manifest Himself by means of other and nobler parts of creation, and use some nobler instrument, such as sun or moon or stars or fire or air, instead of mere man? The answer is this. The Lord did not come to make a display. He came to heal and to teach suffering men. For one who wanted to make a display the thing would have been just to appear and dazzle the beholders. But for Him Who came to heal and to teach the way was not merely to dwell here, but to put Himself at the disposal of those who needed Him, and to be manifested according as they could bear it, not vitiating the value of the Divine appearing by exceeding their capacity to receive it.

Moreover, nothing in creation had erred from the path of God's purpose for it, save only man. Sun, moon, heaven, stars, water, air, none of these had swerved from their order, but, knowing the Word as their Maker and their King, remained as they were made. Men alone having rejected what is good, have invented nothings instead of the truth, and have ascribed the honor due to God and the knowledge concerning Him to demons and men in the form of stones. Obviously the Divine goodness could not overlook so grave a matter as this. But men could not recognize Him as ordering and ruling creation as a whole. So what does He do? He takes to Himself for instrument a part of the whole, namely a human body, and enters into that. Thus He ensured that men should recognize Him in the part who could not do so in the whole, and that those who could not lift their eyes to His unseen power might recognize and behold Him in the likeness of themselves. For, being men, they would naturally learn to know His Father more quickly and directly by means of a body that corresponded to their own and by the Divine works done through it; for by comparing His works with their own they would judge His to be not human but Divine. And if, as they say, it were unsuitable for the Word to reveal Himself through bodily acts, it would be equally so for Him to do so through the works of the universe. His being in creation does not mean that He shares its nature; on the contrary, all created things partake of His power. Similarly, though He used the body as His instrument, He shared nothing of its defect,[1] but rather sanctified it by His indwelling. Does not even Plato, of whom the Greeks think so much, say that the Author of the Universe, seeing it storm-tossed and in danger of sinking into the state of dissolution, takes his seat at the helm of the Life-force of the universe, and comes to the rescue and puts everything right? What, then, is there incredible in our saying that, mankind having gone astray, the Word descended upon it and was manifest as man, so that by His intrinsic goodness and His steersmanship He might save it from the storm?

(44) It may be, however, that, though shamed into agreeing that this objection is void, the Greeks will want to raise another. They will say that, if God wanted to instruct and save mankind, He might have done so, not by His Word's assumption of a body, but, even as He at first created them, by the mere signification of His will. The reasonable reply to that is that the circumstances in the two cases are quite different. In the beginning, nothing as yet existed at all; all that was needed, therefore, in order to bring all things into being, was that His will to do so should be signified. But once man was in existence, and things that were, not things that were not, demanded to be healed, it followed as a matter of course that the Healer and Savior should align Himself with those things that existed already, in order to heal the existing evil. For that reason, therefore, He was made man, and used the body as His human instrument. If this were not the fitting way, and He willed to use an instrument at all, how otherwise was the Word to come? And

[1] Literally, "He shared nothing of the things of the body."

whence could He take His instrument, save from among those already in existence and needing His Godhead through One like themselves? It was not things non-existent that needed salvation, for which a bare creative word might have sufficed, but man-man already in existence and already in process of corruption and ruin. It was natural and right, therefore, for the Word to use a human instrument and by that means unfold Himself to all.

You must know, moreover, that the corruption which had set in was not external to the body but established within it. The need, therefore, was that life should cleave to it in corruption's place, so that, just as death was brought into being in the body, life also might be engendered in it. If death had been exterior to the body, life might fittingly have been the same. But if death was within the body, woven into its very substance and dominating it as though completely one with it, the need was for Life to be woven into it instead, so that the body by thus enduing itself with life might cast corruption off. Suppose the Word had come outside the body instead of in it, He would, of course, have defeated death, because death is powerless against the Life. But the corruption inherent in the body would have remained in it none the less. Naturally, therefore, the Savior assumed a body for Himself, in order that the body, being interwoven as it were with life, should no longer remain a mortal thing, in thrall to death, but as endued with immortality and risen from death, should thenceforth remain immortal. For once having put op corruption, it could not rise, unless it put on life instead; and besides this, death of its very nature could not appear otherwise than in a body. Therefore He put on a body, so that in the body He might find death and blot it out. And, indeed, how could the Lord have been proved to be the Life at all, had He not endued with life that which was subject to death? Take an illustration. Stubble is a substance naturally destructible by fire; and it still remains stubble, fearing the menace of fire which has the natural property of consuming it, even if fire is kept away from it, so that it is not actually burnt. But suppose that, instead of merely keeping the fire from it somebody soaks the stubble with a quantity of asbestos, the substance which is said to be the antidote to fire. Then the stubble no longer fears the fire, because it has put on that which fire cannot touch, and therefore it is safe. It is just the same with regard to the body and death. Had death been kept from it by a mere command, it would still have remained mortal and corruptible, according to its nature. To prevent this, it put on the incorporeal Word of God, and therefore fears neither death nor corruption any more, for it is clad with Life as with a garment and in it corruption is clean done away.

(45) The Word of God thus acted consistently in assuming a body and using a human instrument to vitalize the body. He was consistent in working through man to reveal Himself everywhere, as well as through the other parts of His creation, so that nothing was left void of His Divinity and knowledge. For I take up now the point I made before, namely that the Savior did this in order that He might fill all things everywhere with the knowledge of Himself, just as they are already filled with His presence, even as the Divine Scripture says, "The whole universe was filled with the knowledge of the Lord."[1] If a man looks up to heaven he sees there His ordering; but if he cannot look so high as heaven, but only so far as men, through His works he sees His power, incomparable with human might, and learns from them that He alone among men is God the Word. Or, if a man has gone astray among demons and is in fear of them, he may see this Man drive them out and judge therefrom that He is indeed their Master. Again, if a man has been immersed in the element of water and thinks that it is God—as indeed the Egyptians do worship water—he may see its very nature changed by Him and learn that the Lord is Creator of all. And if a man has gone down even to Hades, and stands awestruck before the heroes who have descended thither, regarding them as gods, still he may see the fact of Christ's resurrection and His victory over death, and reason from it that, of all these, He alone is very Lord and God.

For the Lord touched all parts of creation, and freed and undeceived them all from every deceit. As St. Paul says, "Having put off from Himself the principalities and the powers, He triumphed on the cross,"[2] so that no one could possibly be any longer deceived, but everywhere might find the very Word of God. For thus man, enclosed on every side by the works of creation and everywhere—in heaven, in Hades, in men

---

1 Isaiah 11:9

2 Colossians 2:15

and on the earth, beholding the unfolded Godhead of the Word, is no longer deceived concerning God, but worships Christ alone, and through Him rightly knows the Father.

On these grounds, then, of reason and of principle, we will fairly silence the Gentiles in their turn. But if they think these arguments insufficient to confute them, we will go on in the next chapter to prove our point from facts.

# 8

## Refutation of the Gentiles—Continued

(46) When did people begin to abandon the worship of idols, unless it were since the very Word of God came among men? When have oracles ceased and become void of meaning, among the Greeks and everywhere, except since the Savior has revealed Himself on earth? When did those whom the poets call gods and heroes begin to be adjudged as mere mortals, except when the Lord took the spoils of death and preserved incorruptible the body He had taken, raising it from among the dead? Or when did the deceitfulness and madness of demons fall under contempt, save when the Word, the Power of God, the Master of all these as well, condescended on account of the weakness of mankind and appeared on earth? When did the practice and theory of magic begin to be spurned under foot, if not at the manifestation of the Divine Word to men? In a word, when did the wisdom of the Greeks become foolish, save when the true Wisdom of God revealed Himself on earth? In old times the whole world and every place in it was led astray by the worship of idols, and men thought the idols were the only gods that were. But now all over the world men are forsaking the fear of idols and taking refuge with Christ; and by worshipping Him as God they come through Him to know the Father also, Whom formerly they did not know. The amazing thing, moreover, is this. The objects of worship formerly were varied and countless; each place had its own idol and the so-called god of one place could not pass over to another in order to persuade the people there to worship him, but was barely reverenced even by his own. Indeed no! Nobody worshipped his neighbor's god, but every man had his own idol and thought that it was lord of all. But now Christ alone

is worshipped, as One and the Same among all peoples everywhere; and what the feebleness of idols could not do, namely, convince even those dwelling close at hand, He has effected. He has persuaded not only those close at hand, but literally the entire world to worship one and the same Lord and through Him the Father.

(47) Again, in former times every place was full of the fraud of the oracles, and the utterances of those at Delphi and Dordona and in Boeotia and Lycia and Libya and Egypt and those of the Kabiri and the Pythoness were considered marvelous by the minds of men. But now, since Christ has been proclaimed everywhere, their madness too has ceased, and there is no one left among them to give oracles at all. Then, too, demons used to deceive men's minds by taking up their abode in springs or rivers or trees or stones and imposing upon simple people by their frauds. But now, since the Divine appearing of the Word, all this fantasy has ceased, for by the sign of the cross, if a man will but use it, he drives out their deceits. Again, people used to regard as gods those who are mentioned in the poets—Zeus and Kronos and Apollo and the heroes, and in worshipping them they went astray. But now that the Savior has appeared among men, those others have been exposed as mortal men, and Christ alone is recognized as true God, Word of God, God Himself. And what is one to say about the magic that they think so marvellous? Before the sojourn of the Word, it was strong and active among Egyptians and Chaldeans and Indians and filled all who saw it with terror and astonishment. But by the coming of the Truth and the manifestation of the Word it too has been confuted and entirely destroyed. As to Greek wisdom, however, and the philosophers' noisy talk, I really think no one requires argument from us; for the amazing fact is patent to all that, for all that they had written so much, the Greeks failed to convince even a few from their own neighborhood in regard to immortality and the virtuous ordering of life. Christ alone, using common speech and through the agency of men not clever with their tongues, has convinced whole assemblies of people all the world over to despise death, and to take heed to the things that do not die, to look past the things of time and gaze on things eternal, to think nothing of earthly glory and to aspire only to immortality.

(48) These things which we have said are no mere words: they are attested by actual experience. Anyone who likes may see the proof

of glory in the virgins of Christ, and in the young men who practice chastity as part of their religion, and in the assurance of immortality in so great and glad a company[1] of martyrs. Anyone, too, may put what we have said to the proof of experience in another way. In the very presence of the fraud of demons and the imposture of the oracles and the wonders of magic, let him use the sign of the cross which they all mock at, and but speak the Name of Christ, and he shall see how through Him demons are routed, oracles cease, and all magic and witchcraft is confounded.

Who, then, is this Christ and how great is He, Who by His Name and presence overshadows and confounds all things on every side, Who alone is strong against all and has filled the whole world with His teaching? Let the Greeks tell us, who mock at Him without stint or shame. If He is a man, how is it that one man has proved stronger than all those whom they themselves regard as gods, and by His own power has shown them to be nothing? If they call Him a magician, how is it that by a magician all magic is destroyed, instead of being rendered strong? Had He conquered certain magicians or proved Himself superior to one of them only, they might reasonably think that He excelled the rest only by His greater skill. But the fact is that His cross has vanquished all magic entirely and has conquered the very name of it. Obviously, therefore, the Savior is no magician, for the very demons whom the magicians invoke flee from Him as from their Master. Who is He, then? Let the Greeks tell us, whose only serious pursuit is mockery! Perhaps they will say that He, too, is a demon, and that is why He prevailed. But even so the laugh is still on our side. for we can confute them by the same proofs as before. How could He be a demon, Who drives demons out? If it were only certain ones that He drove out, then they might reasonably think that He prevailed against them through the power of their Chief, as the Jews, wishing to insult Him, actually said. But since the fact is, here again, that at the mere naming of His Name all madness of the demons is rooted out and put to flight, obviously the Greeks are

---

1 Literally, "so great a chorus . . ." "choros" being properly a band of dancers and singers.

wrong here, too, and our Lord and Savior Christ is not, as they maintain, some demonic power.

If, then, the Savior is neither a mere man nor a magician, nor one of the demons, but has by His Godhead confounded and overshadowed the opinions of the poets and the delusion of the demons and the wisdom of the Greeks, it must be manifest and will be owned by all that He is in truth Son of God, Existent Word and Wisdom and Power of the Father. This is the reason why His works are no mere human works, but, both intrinsically and by comparison with those of men, are recognized as being superhuman and truly the works of God.

(49) What man that ever was, for instance, formed a body for himself from a virgin only? Or what man ever healed so many diseases as the common Lord of all? Who restored that which was lacking in man's nature or made one blind from birth to see? Aesculapius was deified by the Greeks because he practiced the art of healing and discovered herbs as remedies for bodily diseases, not, of course, forming them himself out of the earth, but finding them out by the study of nature. But what is that in comparison with what the Savior did when, instead of just healing a wound, He both fashioned essential being and restored to health the thing that He had formed? Hercules, too, is worshipped as a god by the Greeks because he fought against other men and destroyed wild animals by craft. But what is that to what the Word did, in driving away from men diseases and demons and even death itself? Dionysus is worshipped among them, because he taught men drunkenness; yet they ridicule the true Savior and Lord of all, Who taught men temperance.

That, however, is enough on this point. What will they say to the other marvels of His Godhead? At what man's death was the sun darkened and the earth shaken? Why, even to this day men are dying, and they did so also before that time. When did any such marvels happen in their case? Now shall we pass over the deeds done in His earthly body and mention those after His resurrection? Has any man's teaching, in any place or at any time, ever prevailed everywhere as one and the same, from one end of the earth to the other, so that his worship has fairly flown through every land? Again, if, as they say, Christ is man only and not God the Word, why do not the gods of the Greeks prevent

His entering their domains? Or why, on the other hand, does the Word Himself dwelling in our midst make an end of their worship by His teaching and put their fraud to shame?

(50) Many before Him have been kings and tyrants of the earth, history tells also of many among the Chaldeans and Egyptians and Indians who were wise men and magicians. But which of those, I do not say after his death, but while yet in this life, was ever able so far to prevail as to fill the whole world with his teaching and retrieve so great a multitude from the craven fear of idols, as our Savior has won over from idols to Himself? The Greek philosophers have compiled many works with persuasiveness and much skill in words; but what fruit have they to show for this such as has the cross of Christ? Their wise thoughts were persuasive enough until they died; yet even in their life-time their seeming influence was counterbalanced by their rivalry with one another, for they were a jealous company and declaimed against each other. But the Word of God, by strangest paradox, teaching in meaner language, has put the choicest sophists in the shade, and by confounding their teachings and drawing all men to Himself He has filled His own assemblies. Moreover, and this is the marvellous thing by going down as Man to death He has confounded ail the sounding utterances of the wise men about the idols. For whose death ever drove out demons, or whose death did ever demons fear, save that of Christ? For where the Savior is named, there every demon is driven out. Again, who has ever so rid men of their natural passions that fornicators become chaste and murderers no longer wield the sword and those who formerly were craven cowards boldly play the man? In a word, what persuaded the barbarians and heathen folk in every place to drop their madness and give heed to peace, save the faith of Christ and the sign of the cross? What other things have given men such certain faith in immortality as have the cross of Christ and the resurrection of His body? The Greeks told all sorts of false tales, but they could never pretend that their idols rose again from death: indeed it never entered their heads that a body could exist again after death at all. And one would be particularly ready to listen to them on this point, because by these opinions they have exposed the weakness of their own idolatry, at the same time yielding to Christ the

possibility of bodily resurrection, so that by that means He might be recognized by all as Son of God.

(51) Again, who among men, either after his death or while yet living, taught about virginity and did not account this virtue impossible for human beings? But Christ our Savior and King of all has so prevailed with His teaching on this subject that even children not yet of lawful age promise that virginity which transcends the law. And who among men has ever been able to penetrate even to Scythians and Ethiopians, or Parthians or Armenians or those who are said to live beyond Hyrcania, or even the Egyptians and Chaldeans, people who give heed to magic and are more than naturally enslaved by the fear of demons and savage in their habits, and to preach at all about virtue and self-control and against the worshipping of idols, as has the Lord of all, the Power of God, our Lord Jesus Christ? Yet He not only preached through His own disciples, but also wrought so persuasively on men's understanding that, laying aside their savage habits and forsaking the worship of their ancestral gods, they learnt to know Him and through Him to worship the Father. While they were yet idolaters, the Greeks and Barbarians were always at war with each other, and were even cruel to their own kith and kin. Nobody could travel by land or sea at all unless he was armed with swords, because of their irreconcilable quarrels with each other. Indeed, the whole course of their life was carried on with the weapons, and the sword with them replaced the staff and was the mainstay of all aid. All this time, as I said before, they were serving idols and offering sacrifices to demons, and for all the superstitious awe that accompanied this idol worship, nothing could wean them from that warlike spirit. But, strange to relate, since they came over to the school of Christ, as men moved with real compunction they have laid aside their murderous cruelty and are war-minded no more. On the contrary, all is peace among them and nothing remains save desire for friendship.

(52) Who, then, is He Who has done these things and has united in peace those who hated each other, save the beloved Son of the Father, the common Savior of all, Jesus Christ, Who by His own love underwent all things for our salvation? Even from the beginning, moreover, this peace that He was to administer was foretold, for Scripture says, "They shall beat their swords into ploughshares and their spears into sickles, and nation shall not take sword against nation, neither shall they learn any

more to wage war."[1] Nor is this by any means incredible. The barbarians of the present day are naturally savage in their habits, and as long as they sacrifice to their idols they rage furiously against each other and cannot bear to be a single hour without weapons. But when they hear the teaching of Christ, forthwith they turn from fighting to farming, and instead of arming themselves with swords extend their hands in prayer. In a word, instead of fighting each other, they take up arms against the devil and the demons, and overcome them by their selfcommand and integrity of soul. These facts are proof of the Godhead of the Savior, for He has taught men what they could never learn among the idols. It is also no small exposure of the weakness and nothingness of demons and idols, for it was because they knew their own weakness that the demons were always setting men to fight each other, fearing lest, if they ceased from mutual strife, they would turn to attack the demons themselves. For in truth the disciples of Christ, instead of fighting each other, stand arrayed against demons by their habits and virtuous actions, and chase them away and mock at their captain the devil. Even in youth they are chaste, they endure in times of testing and persevere in toils. When they are insulted, they are patient, when robbed they make light of it, and, marvellous to relate, they make light even of death itself, and become martyrs of Christ.

(53) And here is another proof of the Godhead of the Savior, which is indeed utterly amazing. What mere man or magician or tyrant or king was ever able by himself to do so much? Did anyone ever fight against the whole system of idol-worship and the whole host of demons and all magic and all the wisdom of the Greeks, at a time when all of these were strong and flourishing and taking everybody in, as did our Lord, the very Word of God? Yet He is even now invisibly exposing every man's error, and single-handed is carrying off all men from them all, so that those who used to worship idols now tread them under foot, reputed magicians burn their books and the wise prefer to all studies the interpretation of the gospels. They are deserting those whom formerly they worshipped, they worship and confess as Christ and God Him Whom they used to ridicule as crucified. Their so-called gods are routed by the sign of the

---

1 Isaiah 2:4

cross, and the crucified Savior is proclaimed in all the world as God and Son of God. Moreover, the gods worshipped among the Greeks are now falling into disrepute among them on account of the disgraceful things they did, for those who receive the teaching of Christ are more chaste in life than they. If these, and the like of them, are human works, let anyone who will show us similar ones done by men in former time, and so convince us. But if they are shown to be, and are the works not of men but of God, why are the unbelievers so irreligious as not to recognize the Master Who did them? They are afflicted as a man would be who failed to recognize God the Artificer through the works of creation. For surely if they had recognized His Godhead through His power over the universe, they would recognize also that the bodily works of Christ are not human, but are those of the Savior of all, the Word of God. And had they recognized this, as Paul says, "They would not have crucified the Lord of glory."[1]

(54) As, then, he who desires to see God Who by nature is invisible and not to be beheld, may yet perceive and know Him through His works, so too let him who does not see Christ with his understanding at least consider Him in His bodily works and test whether they be of man or God. If they be of man, then let him scoff; but if they be of God, let him not mock at things which are no fit subject for scorn, but rather let him recognize the fact and marvel that things divine have been revealed to us by such humble means, that through death deathlessness has been made known to us, and through the Incarnation of the Word the Mind whence all things proceed has been declared, and its Agent and Ordainer, the Word of God Himself. He, indeed, assumed humanity that we might become God. He manifested Himself by means of a body in order that we might perceive the Mind of the unseen Father. He endured shame from men that we might inherit immortality. He Himself was unhurt by this, for He is impassable and incorruptible; but by His own impassability He kept and healed the suffering men on whose account He thus endured. In short, such and so many are the Savior's achievements that follow from His Incarnation, that to try to number them is like gazing at the open sea and trying to count the waves. One

---

1 Corinthians 2:8

cannot see all the waves with one's eyes, for when one tries to do so those that are following on baffle one's senses. Even so, when one wants to take in all the achievements of Christ in the body, one cannot do so, even by reckoning them up, for the things that transcend one's thought are always more than those one thinks that one has grasped.

As we cannot speak adequately about even a part of His work, therefore, it will be better for us not to speak about it as a whole. So we will mention but one thing more, and then leave the whole for you to marvel at. For, indeed, everything about it is marvellous, and wherever a man turns his gaze he sees the Godhead of the Word and is smitten with awe.

(55) The substance of what we have said so far may be summarized as follows. Since the Savior came to dwell among us, not only does idolatry no longer increase, but it is getting less and gradually ceasing to be. Similarly, not only does the wisdom of the Greeks no longer make any progress, but that which used to be is disappearing. And demons, so far from continuing to impose on people by their deceits and oracle-givings and sorceries, are routed by the sign of the cross if they so much as try. On the other hand, while idolatry and everything else that opposes the faith of Christ is daily dwindling and weakening and falling, see, the Savior's teaching is increasing everywhere! Worship, then, the Savior "Who is above all" and mighty, even God the Word, and condemn those who are being defeated and made to disappear by Him. When the sun has come, darkness prevails no longer; any of it that may be left anywhere is driven away. So also, now that the Divine epiphany of the Word of God has taken place, the darkness of idols prevails no more, and all parts of the world in every direction are enlightened by His teaching. Similarly, if a king be reigning somewhere, but stays in his own house and does not let himself be seen, it often happens that some insubordinate fellows, taking advantage of his retirement, will have themselves proclaimed in his stead; and each of them, being invested with the semblance of kingship, misleads the simple who, because they cannot enter the palace and see the real king, are led astray by just hearing a king named. When the real king emerges, however, and appears to view, things stand differently. The insubordinate impostors are shown up by his presence, and men, seeing the real king, forsake those who previously misled them. In the same way

the demons used formerly to impose on men, investing themselves with the honor due to God. But since the Word of God has been manifested in a body, and has made known to us His own Father, the fraud of the demons is stopped and made to disappear; and men, turning their eyes to the true God, Word of the Father, forsake the idols and come to know the true God.

Now this is proof that Christ is God, the Word and Power of God. For whereas human things cease and the fact of Christ remains, it is clear to all that the things which cease are temporary, but that He Who remains is God and very Son of God, the sole-begotten Word.

# 9

## Conclusion

(56) Here, then, Macarius, is our offering to you who love Christ, a brief statement of the faith of Christ and of the manifestation of His Godhead to us. This will give you a beginning, and you must go on to prove its truth by the study of the Scriptures. They were written and inspired by God; and we, who have learned from inspired teachers who read the Scriptures and became martyrs for the Godhead of Christ, make further contribution to your eagerness to learn. From the Scriptures you will learn also of His second manifestation to us, glorious and divine indeed, when He shall come not in lowliness but in His proper glory, no longer in humiliation but in majesty, no longer to suffer but to bestow on us all the fruit of His cross—the resurrection and incorruptibility. No longer will He then be judged, but rather will Himself be Judge, judging each and all according to their deeds done in the body, whether good or ill. Then for the good is laid up the heavenly kingdom, but for those that practice evil outer darkness and the eternal fire. So also the Lord Himself says, "I say unto you, hereafter ye shall see the Son of Man seated on the right hand of power, coming on the clouds of heaven in the glory of the Father."[1] For that Day we have one of His own sayings to prepare us, "Get ready and watch, for ye know not the hour in which He cometh"[2] And blessed Paul says, "We must all stand before the judgment seat of

---

1 Matthew 26:64

2 Matthew 24:42

Christ, that each one may receive according as he practiced in the body, whether good or ill."[1]

(57) But for the searching and right understanding of the Scriptures there is need of a good life and a pure soul, and for Christian virtue to guide the mind to grasp, so far as human nature can, the truth concerning God the Word. One cannot possibly understand the teaching of the saints unless one has a pure mind and is trying to imitate their life. Anyone who wants to look at sunlight naturally wipes his eye clear first, in order to make, at any rate, some approximation to the purity of that on which he looks; and a person wishing to see a city or country goes to the place in order to do so. Similarly, anyone who wishes to understand the mind of the sacred writers must first cleanse his own life, and approach the saints by copying their deeds. Thus united to them in the fellowship of life, he will both understand the things revealed to them by God and, thenceforth escaping the peril that threatens sinners in the judgment, will receive that which is laid up for the saints in the kingdom of heaven. Of that reward it is written: "Eye hath not seen nor ear heard, neither hath entered into the heart of man the things that God has prepared"[2] for them that live a godly life and love the God and Father in Christ Jesus our Lord, through Whom and with Whom be to the Father Himself, with the Son Himself, in the Holy Spirit, honor and might and glory to ages of ages.

Amen.

---

1 2 Corinthians 5:10

2 1 Corinthians 2:9